Racquetball:
A Guide for the Aspiring Player

Cheryl Norton, Ed.D.
Assistant Professor of Physical Education
Metropolitan State College, Denver

James E. Bryant, Ed.D.
Professor of Physical Education
Metropolitan State College, Denver

MP
Morton Publishing Company
925 West Kenyon Ave., Unit 4
Englewood, Colorado 80110

Copyright © 1984 by Morton Publishing Company

ISBN 0-89582-112-5

All rights reserved. No part of this publication may be reproduced, stored in a retrieval system, or transmitted, in any form or by any means, electronic, mechanical, photocopying, or otherwise, without prior written permission of the copyright owner.

Acknowledgments

The contributions of several individuals and groups provided the necessary input for completion of this text.

Jane Kober, assistant professor, Metropolitan State College, is acknowledged for her insight and creative thought associated with the chapter on drills for the aspiring player. Ron McCall and Joni McCall contributed the time, skills, and efforts as models for the numerous photographs of skill sequences and play situations. The illustrations, prepared by Darryl Wisnea, added greatly to the understanding of the material concerning various strategies, court dimensions, and drills.

The American Amateur Racquetball Association (AARA) is acknowledged for contributing information related to the resources chapter and for permission to include the official AARA Racquetball Rules in the text. The Aurora Athletic Club is recognized for permitting photographs to be taken of skill and play situations in its club. Hagan Sports Ltd. is acknowledged for permitting photographs to be shot of its racquetball equipment displays.

Preface

Racquetball: A Guide For the Aspiring Player is designed for the beginning and intermediate player who is involved in a learning experience. The text is divided into four sections that deal with various racquetball concepts.

The first six chapters discuss safety, equipment, and skill acquisition and enable the reader to assimilate the needed skills of racquetball into a comprehensive skill attainment package. That package includes fundamentals of movement, assuming the proper grip, and developing skill in the basic offensive and defensive strokes, including passing shots, kill shots, ceiling shots, special strokes, and a variety of serves.

Chapters seven through nine should help the player develop a cognitive approach to playing racquetball. Chapter seven describes a reflex, non-thinking approach to the game for the beginning player, chapter eight presents a thinking approach for the player who can already put the strokes together, and chapter nine deals with the mind and the flow of playing in a relaxed, non-stressful manner.

The third section is physical in nature. Chapter ten presents the physical aspects, including the warm-up, prevention of injuries, fitness qualities provided by racquetball, and nutrition as it relates to the game. Chapter eleven offers an in-depth opportunity for self-improvement through drill practice.

The final three chapters discuss a variety of racquetball information related to court etiquette, interpretation of rules, how to play in tournaments, and where to go for information after the lessons are completed. They also relate how the game has developed in recent years and how society responds to racquetball.

Additional features include a unique mini-division of questions asked by aspiring racquetball players, a self-appraisal checklist of skill and mental preparation, and a glossary of terms important to racquetball participants.

The text is an appropriate guide for the aspiring racquetball player and will help him/her to develop both physical and mental skills needed to be successful in the game. Through the use of extensive, quality photographs and illustrations, the concept of the game as a comprehensive, artistic, physical activity is advanced. The learning experiences, including "points to remember" and "common errors and why you make them," are helpful learning devices that will provide more in-depth knowledge of a player's own skills. In total, the text provides a professional learning experience for the serious racquetball student.

Table of Contents

Acknowledgments		i
Preface		iii
Chapter One	— Court, Equipment, and Safety	1
Chapter Two	— Introduction and Preliminaries to the Strokes in Racquetball	13
Chapter Three	— Offensive Strokes	33
Chapter Four	— Defensive Strokes	49
Chapter Five	— Serves in Racquetball	63
Chapter Six	— Special Strokes and Shots	79
Chapter Seven	— Putting the Strokes Together: Non-Thinking Strategy	93
Chapter Eight	— Putting the Strokes Together: Thinking Strategy	105
Chapter Nine	— Mental Aspects of Racquetball	121
Chapter Ten	— Physical Aspects of Racquetball	133
Chapter Eleven	— Drills for the Aspiring Player	153
Chapter Twelve	— Court Etiquette and Interpreting the Rules	165
Chapter Thirteen	— Resources in Racquetball	181
Chapter Fourteen	— The Foundations of Racquetball	187
Glossary of Terms in Racquetball		191
The Aspiring Racquetball Player's Self-Appraisal Checklist		195
The American Amateur Racquetball Rules		199
Index		213

Chapter One

Court, Equipment, and Safety

Racquetball is played in an enclosed court using the four walls, floor, and ceiling as the playing surface. In areas where a four-wall court cannot be built, one- or three-wall racquetball may be played. The rules and strategy for all of these games are similar. This text, however, will concentrate only on the more complex, four-wall racquetball.

The walls of the court may be made of any one of several types of materials from cement to glass. The most commonly used material is prefabricated resin board. However, glass is becoming more popular as racquetball assumes more of a spectator-sport following. Any type of floor may be played on, but a wooden floor is used for tournament play.

The dimensions and markings on the court are specified by the official rules of the game (see page 199). Fortunately, the terminology used to describe the court is easily learned: floor, ceiling, front, back, and side walls. The floor lines identify the *service zone* boundaries. The only other mark on the court denotes the *receiving line* for the player returning the serve.

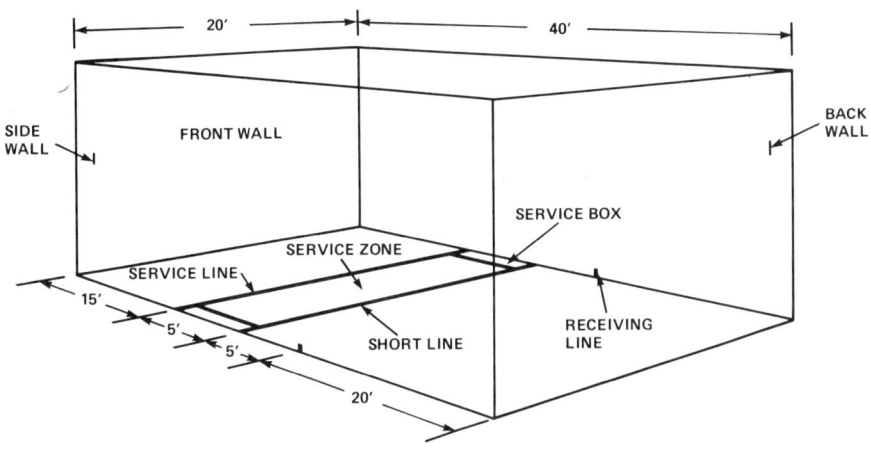

Dimensions and markings on a racquetball court.

The court can also be divided into four main areas of play.

Designated floor areas on the court.

Brief Overview of the Game

The object of the game of racquetball is to score 21 points before your opponent does. Only the serving player scores points. A point is scored when the server's opponent fails to hit the ball to the front wall before the ball touches the floor twice. If the server fails to return the ball to the front wall, he/she loses serve. In this way, service (and the opportunity to score) is alternated until one player or team accumulates 21 points and wins the game.

Racquetball may be played with two (singles), three (cut-throat), or four (doubles) players. In singles, one player opposes another player, and in doubles, one two-person team plays another two-person team. However, in cut-throat, a single server plays against two opponents. When the server loses serve, one of the opponents becomes the server and plays against the remaining two players. The first player to earn 21 points during his/her serve is the winner.

In all games, each rally (exchange of hits between opposing players) is begun with a *legal serve*. For the serve to be legal, the server must stand in the service zone, drop the ball to the floor, and strike it on the rebound so that it hits the front wall first. The front wall rebound can only touch the floor behind the short line. Before the ball hits the floor, it may rebound off one side wall but not off the ceiling, back wall, or both side walls. However, the return of serve and any other hit can rebound the ball off any surface except the floor before reaching the front wall. Service is changed when the server fails to keep the ball in play or he/she does not serve legally. If the receiver fails to return the ball to the front wall, a point is scored.

Outfitting for Play

Dress: The most important rule for dress is to be comfortable and wear clothes that allow for the release of body heat. In a fast-moving game like racquetball, body temperature increases rapidly. The result of overheating the body through exercising and wearing tight-fitting clothes is general body fatigue, slower reaction times, and dehydration. Therefore, loose-fitting, natural fiber clothes that allow air to circulate and cool are the dress of preference. In addition, loose-fitting clothes allow for maximum body movement. The usual dress for both men and women includes a sports shirt or T-shirt and shorts. All clothes must be white or light colored. The rules of play forbid dark colors, since they may interfere with the sighting of the ball.

Proper dress for racquetball.

Head or wristbands aid in the absorption of perspiration around the head and hands and are optional to wear. Shirts will help to absorb body perspiration and must be worn at all times during play. Body perspiration dripping onto the floor of the court provides a potential hazard to fast-moving feet.

Shoes: Foot comfort and support are of utmost concern. A good-fitting shoe with adequate lateral support can alleviate many problems with blisters and muscle/joint irritation. This means that shoes designed for jogging/running should *not* be worn on the racquetball court. First, many of these shoes have a black sole, which mars the surface of wooden floors. Second, the support in these shoes is designed for straight-line movement and provides very little ankle support for stop-start activity or quick lateral foot adjustments. The footwear worn on a racquetball court should be an athletic shoe that will support shifting body weight and position on the court. Finally, adequate socks or foot cover will prevent the foot from sliding in the shoe and irritating the skin.

Racquetball head and wrist bands.

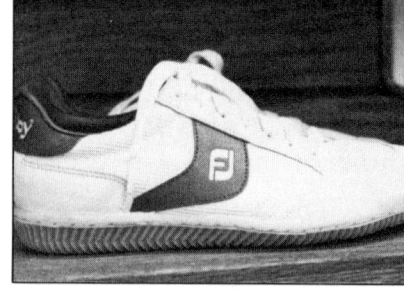

Athletic shoe suitable for racquetball.

Gloves: The use of a glove is optional and dependent upon your comfort and need. Many players wear a glove on their racquet hand to help maintain a better grip on the racquet and prevent the racquet from slipping from their hand. Gloves are made of synthetic materials and/or leather. Any glove the you choose should be light, flexible, soft, and thin to allow you to maintain the "feel" of the racquet. Thus, a glove should feel like a "second skin" but allow the hand and the grip of the racquet to stay dry. Having several pairs of gloves will allow you to wear one while the other is drying out, thus prolonging the life of each glove.

Goggles: Although protective eyewear is not regulated through the official rules of racquetball, many courts maintain a policy of having to wear goggles to play. Severe eye damage, including detached retinas and the loss of vision, have followed direct eye hits with either the ball or the racquet. Goggles can be bought to wear over eyeglasses or to protect the eye itself. For some players,

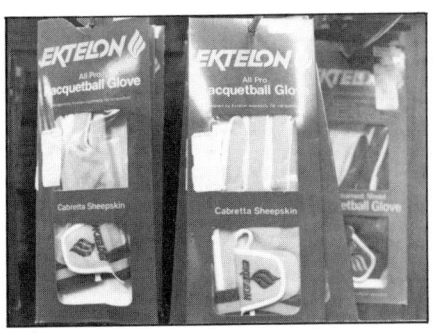
Racquetball gloves.

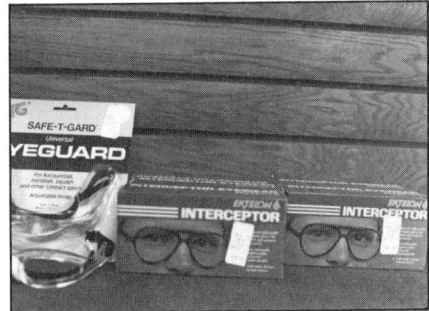
Protective goggles.

goggles feel uncomfortable. Make sure that you have tried several types of goggles, from the wraparound to the form-fitting style, to find one that is the best fit for you. In addition, anti-fogging products can be purchased to coat the lens surface and prevent clouding.

Ball: Specifications for a racquetball ball are outlined in the rules of the game (see page 200). Balls usually cost between $1.00 and $3.00. They can be purchased at sporting goods stores as well

Racquetball balls.

as at most discount stores that carry athletic equipment. Balls come in either black, red, green, or blue. Choose the color that your eyes follow the best.

Recently, pressurized balls that can be inflated to a specified pressure have been used in games. Consequently, they are often overinflated and are very "lively" during play. Beginning players should not learn the game of racquetball with this type of ball. More advanced players may find that these balls provide an exciting and fast game. Keep in mind, though, that the pressure of balls used in tournament play is very closely regulated and may not be the same as what you have practiced with if a pressurized ball was used.

Racquets: The selection of a racquet is dependent upon your style of play and the amount of money you want to invest. The frame of a racquet is either constructed of a metal such as aluminum or steel or is a composite of high-technology fibers such as graphite, boron, and fiberglass. The metal racquets cost less to

Selection of racquets.

make and are usually more durable but do not have the flexibility of the composite racquet. Because of their stiffness, aluminum racquets are more popular for players who choose a power game over a controlled "placement" game. The composite racquets, on the other hand, are flexible and keep the ball on the strings longer, thus providing more control over ball placement.

Both types of racquets are very light in weight, usually tipping the scale at between 8 and 10 ounces. The less arm strength you have, the lighter the racquet you should use. A lighter racquet allows you to swing faster, react more quickly, and experience less arm fatigue during play. For these reasons, women generally choose a lighter racquet than men.

Grip Size: As a rule of thumb, the grip size should be smaller than that of a tennis racquet. Most experts suggest that when gripping the racquet properly, the middle finger of the racquet hand should just touch the palm to allow for a good wrist snap. However, tennis players who have become racquetball players often find this grip uncomfortably small. Choose a grip that "feels" good to you. However, if you choose a larger grip, you will lose some wrist snap in your swing and consequently have less power in your stroke. If you buy a grip size that feels small to you, although it technically fits correctly, you can always build up the grip size if necessary. Play with the racquet before you make your decision.

Racquet Strings and Tension: Racquets are usually already strung when you buy them. The two types of materials commonly used to make strings are nylon and gut. Gut has very little advantage over a good nylon string. If anything, gut tends to wear out faster and must be replaced more often. Therefore, the additional price of gut usually does not provide you with additional quality. Gut strings do help to put spin on the ball, but spin is not a critical factor in racquetball.

If you must have your racquet restrung, you can specify the amount of tension in the strings. Tension levels vary from 23 pounds (fiberglass racquets) to 33 or 35 pounds (metal racquets). On the average, most players opt for a tension level between 26 and 28 pounds. The more tension on the racquet strings, the faster the ball will rebound off the racquet; consequently, the more control the player must have to accurately place the ball. Therefore, beginning players who have trouble controlling shots should string their racquets with less tension.

Handle and Thong: Racquet handles are made of rubber or leather. Although leather is more expensive, it usually allows you to grip the racquet more securely. If you are buying a used racquet, check to see if the frame extends to the end of the handle. On some older, cheaper racquets, the frame was only inserted into the grip. This type of construction will usually break down more quickly than if the frame extends the length of the handle.

To be legal, each racquet must have a *thong* attached to the handle. The thong is a safety cord that is worn on the wrist during play. Replacement thongs may be purchased where racquetball equipment is supplied.

Care: Racquets are easy to care for if you use some common sense. Try not to leave your racquet in the backseat of your car. Extremes in heat or cold will cause the strings to become brittle or break down faster. Keep a cover on the racquet to prevent objects from catching in the strings. If your strings are breaking frequently, you can have plastic eyelets inserted where the string wraps around the frame to protect the strings from wearing on the edge. Finally, any racquet if hit into a side or back wall often will break. Learn to

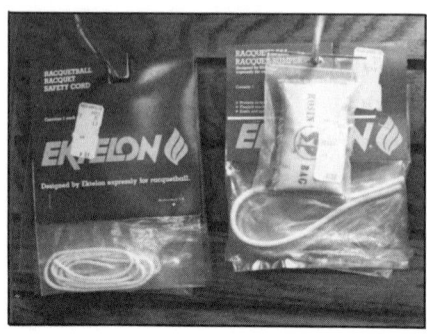

Replacement safety thongs.

play racquetball correctly, and use your racquet to hit the ball rather than a wall.

New racquets come with a guidebook. Familiarize yourself with the manufacturer's suggestions about the care and use of the racquet. This booklet usually includes a warranty card. Be sure to send it in as soon as possible to protect your investment.

Safety on the Court

Safety on the court begins when you walk onto the court, put on your goggles, and shut the door to protect against people walking in during play. During play, a racquetball court is safe only if all the players are courteous. This means staying out of your opponent's path to the ball or arm swing. Similarly, no shot is "too good to pass up" if a player is in the path of your swing. There is no excuse for hitting another player with your racquet. If he/she were

Hitting a ball when your opponent is in the way.

that close to you, your shot could not have been clear. In addition, learn to play the strokes correctly. Too many players keep their tennis stroke alive in the racquetball court. Wide swings from the shoulder require the room that a tennis court provides. There is no place on the racquetball court for this kind of play.

As mentioned above, each racquet must have a thong or safety cord attached to it. This cord is worn around the wrist of the playing hand to prevent the racquet from flying out of the hand of the player and injuring someone on the court. This cord must be used at all times.

Finally, you should continually be aware of what is happening on the court. Stay out of the way of the player hitting the ball, and when it is your turn to hit, take your shot only if it is clear. However, most balls are hit from the back of the court forward. If you are in front of the ball, DO NOT turn completely around to "see" what is going on behind you in the back court. This not only exposes your chest and abdomen to a hard-hit ball, but it leaves your face unprotected. Rather, you should angle your body slightly so that you can see the back court with your peripheral vision and hold up the racquet to protect your face as you look through the strings. Using the racquet to protect your face from an oncoming ball is an effective safety measure only if the racquet "beats" the ball to the target. Don't rely on your reflexes to "get the racquet" up in

Protecting your face by looking through the racquet strings.

time to protect your face. As a precaution, always use your racquet as a shield if your face is exposed to the ball's path, and wear your goggles to protect your eyes against the stray shot. This way you can play the game and finish "looking" the same way as when you entered the court.

Inevitably, some players will become so intrigued by the challenge of the game that they will sacrifice their bodies just to "get to the ball." This results in bodily contact with side walls, the back wall, and even the floor. This contact occurs when you run through the stroke and into a wall while chasing the ball around the court, or when you dive onto the floor in order to "save" a ball. Beginning players are more likely to collide with the court walls than experienced players. This is simply because beginners are often out of position in relation to the ball and must run to "catch" it, and they are unable to stop before contacting the court. Fortunately, with a little care these "collisions" can be made without serious injury. The secret is to hit the surface and roll in the direction of your momentum. The rolling motion along a wall usually occurs along the upper back with your hand pushing off from the wall when the roll is complete. When diving for a ball, try

Hitting the ball and protecting yourself by rolling off the wall.

to absorb the force of the fall with your chest and upper body. If possible, avoid landing on your knees or elbows, since little covering is there to cushion the fall. Ideally, contact with the walls or floor

Diving for a ball.

should not have to be made. This type of desperation shot should only be considered when no other shot is possible, and even then you need to seriously consider if winning the point is worth possible injury.

A player can also run into his/her opponent, at times resulting in serious injury. The best way to avoid colliding with your opponent is by being aware of where the ball and the opponent are at all times. If your opponent is moving for the ball, give him/her the right-of-way before repositioning yourself. You should be aware that experienced players will let the ball rebound off the back wall before playing it. This means that a center court position needs to be held open for him/her to follow the ball. Anticipate the most

Player not leaving center court to give opponent clear shot off a back wall rebound.

direct path to the ball that your opponent can take, and keep that court position clear. Racquetball is not a game that allows mental lapses. Each player must know where the ball is at all times and where other players are moving.

Another serious safety problem occurs when a player tries to return the ball to the front wall by hitting it first into the back wall. Although hitting into the back wall is legal, it is an ineffective hit and in most cases presents a danger on the court. If the player hitting into the back wall is only 1 to 3 feet from the wall, often the ball rebounds off this surface and into the face of the hitter. If the hitter is standing in mid or center court when the ball is hit, usually the opposing player is between this court position and the back wall. Consequently, the opponent is facing a ball hit directly at him/her. With a hard-hit ball, it is difficult to get out of the way, especially because this hit is unexpected. Trying to hit the ball backward to go forward prevents a player from directing the ball accurately. It also reduces the speed and power of the hit because of the distance the ball travels. Hitting into the back wall, then, not only creates safety problems on the court but is a weak shot at best and should be discouraged.

Safety is a matter of habit and thinking: protect yourself by wearing goggles, using your racquet as a shield, keeping your thong on your wrist, and closing the door of the court when playing. Anticipate your opponent's position, the path of the ball, and the movement of players on the court. Most important, remember that racquetball is just a game, and one point is not worth risking your health or that of your opponent just to "make a shot."

Chapter Two

Introduction and Preliminaries to the Strokes in Racquetball

The preliminaries to the strokes in racquetball are specific to the execution of offensive and defensive shots. These preliminaries include the warm-up, how to grip the racquet, assuming the set or ready position, the pivot to hit the ball, the forehand stroke, and the backhand stroke.

Getting Ready to Participate: the Warm-Up

A good rule of thumb to follow for any exercise in which you engage is "never take your body by surprise." A warm-up to prepare yourself mentally and physically allows your body to smoothly "shift gears" from inactivity to activity. The stress of sudden activity causes your body to rely on reserve energy sources rather than energy derived from breathing oxygen. Using up your reserve energy at the start of the exercise means that you will fatigue more quickly, and you will have to quit the activity or your level of play will decline.

The warm-up should consist of three phases: relaxation, stretching, and increased heart activity. Relaxation is needed to relieve internal stress. The body responds to stress by increasing muscle tension. Tight muscles work in opposition to the free and fluid movement needed for any exercise/sport activity. In addition, stretching exercises will be more effective if the muscles are relaxed.

Stretching is the second phase of the warm-up. It is important to help increase your ease and range of movement. Since racquetball is literally a game of inches, the ability to extend your reach to its limit may "make up" for slowly reacting to the ball's action.

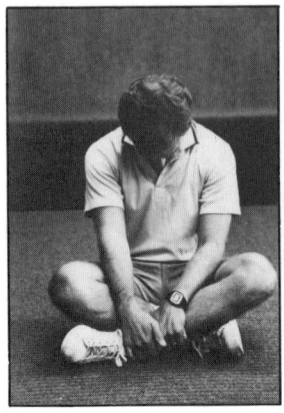 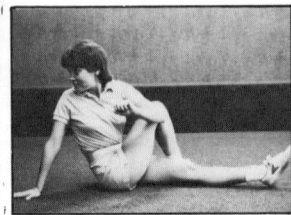 

Getting ready to play: relaxing, stretching, increasing your heart rate.

Another important function of this phase is to help alleviate residual soreness from previous racquetball sessions and avoid further injury to tight muscles that may have resulted from the sudden movements required by the game.

The last phase of the warm-up should increase your heart rate, since this activity will also increase the body's energy liberation. As a result, at the beginning of the game, the reserve energy stores are not depleted. Playing racquetball will "feel" more comfortable, and you will not tire as rapidly.

These three warm-up activities are done in sequence immediately before entering the court to play. Many people make the mistake of warming up and then waiting for 5 to 10 minutes before playing racquetball. Consequently, most of the effect of the warm-up is lost. The increase in heart rate will decline within one to two minutes after the warm-up is over. Therefore, no time should be wasted getting onto the court.

Activities that you can use to relax, stretch, and increase your heart rate are outlined in Chapter 10. Listen to your body. If after you go through these exercises, you still do not feel ready to play, do some more. Each day is not the same, and your body is constantly changing. Learn to know how you "feel" when you are "warmed-up."

Last but not least is mental preparation for play. Unless your mind is relaxed and focused on the sport ahead, your body cannot respond properly to the challenge of the game. Chapter 9 focuses on the mental aspects of racquetball and on preparing yourself mentally to play. Without proper mental preparation, your skills cannot be used to their fullest.

Holding the Racquet: the Grips

The power in a racquetball stroke comes from the snap of the wrist that occurs when the ball is contacted. Unless the racquet is gripped in such a way as to maximize this snap, the potential power of a stroke will be lost. There are two basic grips that most players adapt to their style of play and a third that some use in special situations. The first, and easily the most popular, is the Eastern Forehand. The Eastern Forehand, as its name implies, is used to hit only shots on the racquet-hand (forehand) side of the body. Its counterpart on the non-racquet-hand side is the Eastern Backhand and will be discussed later.

The easiest way to assume an Eastern Forehand grip is merely to hold the racquet on edge so that it is perpendicular to the floor and then "shake hands" with the handle. In the shaking hands

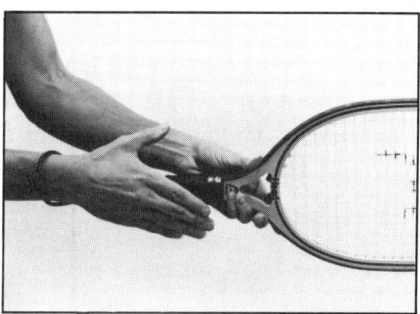

Shaking hands with the racquet.

position, the first finger and thumb of the racquet hand should form a "V" along the top of the racquet, the point of the "V" lying on the midline of the handle's surface. The fingers are spread in a "trigger or pistol grip" position to allow for better wrist snap.

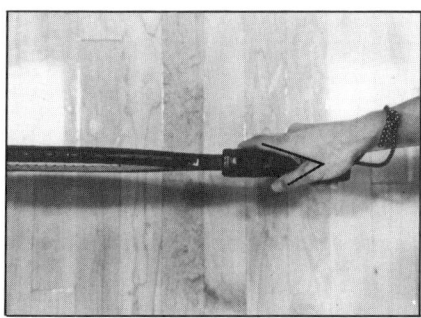

Eastern Forehand Grip.

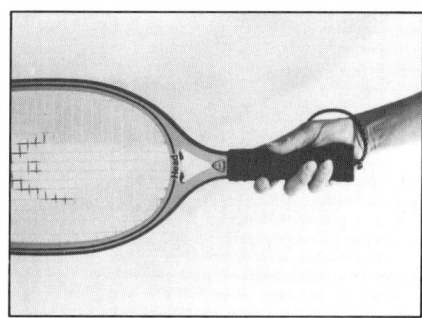

Trigger or Finger Grip.

Another way to assume this position is to hold the racquet in the non-racquet hand so that the racquet is again on edge. Place your racquet hand with fingers spread on the strings of the racquet so that the palm is flat against the racquet face. Slide your racquet

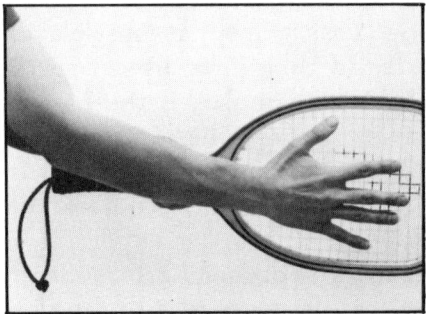

Palm flat on racquet face.

hand down the racquet until the end of the handle meets the end of your palm, and wrap your fingers around the handle. Again you should check to see if the "V" formed by your first finger and thumb is pointed properly along the top surface of the handle. Be careful not to grip the racquet so that the handle lies perpendicular to your fingers in a "fist" grip or the wrist snap will be lost. If you

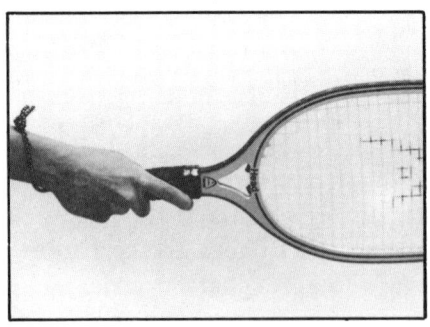

Assuming the Eastern Forehand grip.

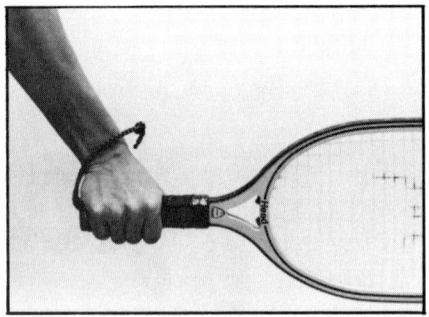

Improper grip on racquet, fingers perpendicular to handle.

turn the racquet over so that your palm is pointed toward the ceiling of the court and open your hand, a racquet in the correct position should lie diagonally across the palm. The handle should cover the first knuckle of the first finger and the bottom left side of the palm.

If you use this grip for your forehand shots, you must change your grip to hit backhand shots (shots to the non-racquet-hand

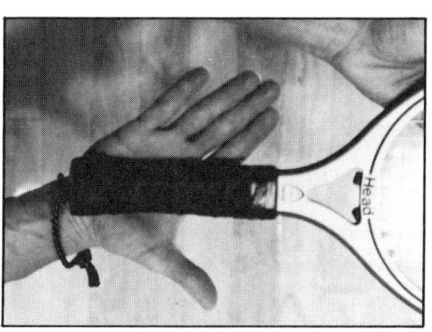

Handle of racquet lies diagonally across palm of hand.

side). This is due to the way in which the arm moves about the elbow. The construction of the elbow joint causes the forearm to move only up and down (flex and extend) when the arm is held straight at your side. When hitting a backhand shot, the racquet arm is pulled across the body and then extended. If the hand is held in its normal position in line with the elbow, the racquet head will be turned up and will hit the ball at an angle with the extension. Thus, shots that should be hit straight into the wall will be "popped," or hit up toward the ceiling. To hit a level backhand shot, you must change your grip from the Eastern Forehand to the Eastern Backhand grip. To find this position on your racquet, assume the forehand grip just discussed and hold the racquet on edge. With your non-racquet hand, turn the top of the racquet toward the palm of your hand so that the forefinger-thumb "V" falls below the top left edge of the racquet. This grip rotates the

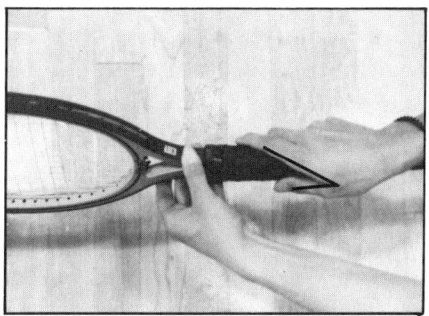

Eastern Backhand Grip.

head of the racquet downward to compensate for the elbow's inability to rotate and allows you to hit a level ball. The problem with changing from the forehand to the backhand grip is that it takes TIME. Thus, it is important that you immediately recognize when a backhand shot should be hit to give you as much time as possible to make the switch. A similar problem occurs after the backhand shot is taken. The grip must be changed back to the forehand placement. Unfortunately, many players have difficulty changing grips and hitting the ball too! But a player must do something to change the angle of the racquet head!

One alternative solution to this problem is to simply rotate the wrist forward when hitting a backhand shot. This turns the racquet head downward and allows a flat shot to be hit. Returning to the

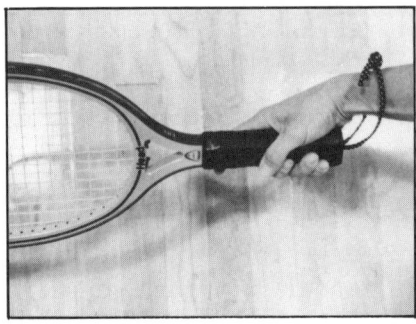

Rotating wrist forward to turn racquet face down.

Eastern Forehand grip only takes a "twist" of the wrist. The major problem with this method is that it is so easy, new players often FORGET to do it!

Either way of changing the racquet position for a backhand can be effective as long as you consistently use it. Choose one method and practice with it all the time.

A second alternative to changing grips is to avoid using the Eastern Forehand and Backhand grips completely. Instead, use the Continental grip. In the Continental grip, the racquet is held in a position midway between the Eastern Forehand and Backhand. To assume this grip, the racquet must be rotated one-eighth of a turn from the Eastern Forehand toward the forehand side. Now the "V" will point to the top left edge of the handle. Thus, with the

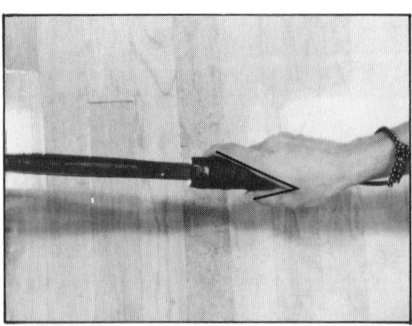

Continental Grip.

Continental grip, little or no adjustment must be made for either a forehand or backhand shot, although the wrist may be slightly rotated clockwise to adjust the face of the racquet to hit a level ball.

The third grip is called the Western grip or "frying pan" grip. It is similar to the grip you use on a frying pan handle when you lift the pan off a stove or pick your racquet up off the floor. This grip is

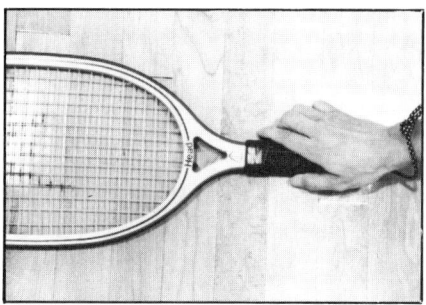 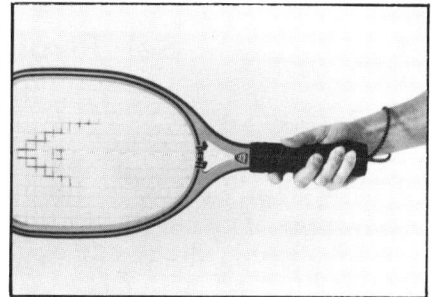

Western Grip.

used ONLY for overhead forehand shots. However, new players often use this grip on all shots and consequently have difficulty hitting low balls.

After hitting a few balls, always recheck your grip to make sure that the racquet has not twisted in your hand. Some players will even mark the "V" placement of the thumb and forefinger on the racquet's top edge with tape. This helps to guide the correct hand positioning.

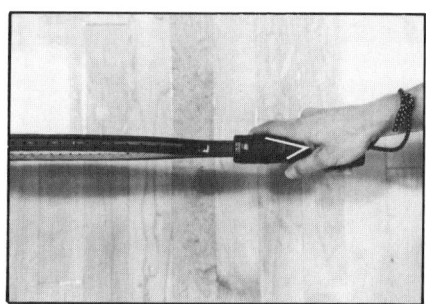

Eastern Forehand Grip marked with a "V" on the racquet.

Points to Remember:

1. Note the position of the "V" on the racquet handle and make sure that it matches your hand placement.
2. Keep your fingers spread out in a pistol or trigger finger grip — do not keep a fist grip on the handle.

3. Change to a backhand grip or compensate for the elbow's movement by rotating the wrist to hit a ball on the non-racquet side. Change back to a forehand grip after the shot has been taken.
4. Overhead shots may be hit using a Western grip.
5. Continental grip may be used to hit all balls.

Set, Pivot, and Stroke

The Set

The set or "ready" position prepares you to hit the ball. Begin each stroke at the set position and return to it following each hit. The set position allows you to move quickly to hit a ball with either your forehand or backhand.

To get in the set position, stand with your feet shoulder width apart, toes pointing forward and weight equally balanced on the balls of the feet. The racquet should be held in front of you at waist height, and a forehand grip should be used. Your non-racquet hand should help to support the racquet. Knees should be slightly bent and pointed forward. Shoulders, head, and neck are relaxed, with your eyes free to follow the movement of the ball. Breathing must be deep and regular.

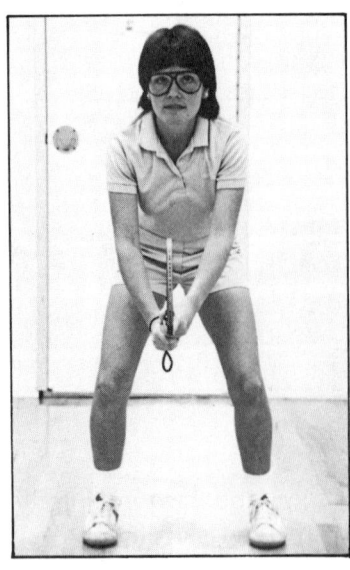

Set Position — front view.   Set Position — side view.

Points to Remember:

1. Face the front wall, with toes pointed forward.
2. Weight is equally balanced on the balls of the feet, which are placed shoulder width apart.
3. Hold the racquet with a forehand grip at waist height in front of you.
4. Knees are bent, and the body is ready to "spring" into action.

The Pivot

As soon as you have decided if the ball is to be hit with a forehand or backhand stroke, you must PIVOT or turn your body to prepare for the hit. The sooner the decision can be made, the better prepared you will be to hit the ball. So decide QUICKLY. The importance of the pivot is that it turns the hips sideways to the front wall. This allows for the player to "step into" the ball and add his/her body weight into the power of the stroke. A baseball batter

Pivot position for forehand stroke.

Stepping into the ball from a pivot position.

will take the same position. Except to bunt, the batter will always stand sideways to the pitcher and step into the pitch by shifting his weight forward. Thus, the ball can be hit with more force. Similarly, the pivot in racquetball positions you to step into the ball, shift your weight, and increase the power of your stroke. This is especially important for women players who may have weak arms and wrists.

The pivot itself may be done in either of two ways. In both methods, you must put your weight on one foot and turn on that foot to face a side wall. Your free foot will either be pulled forward or behind you to complete the pivot. In either case, your body

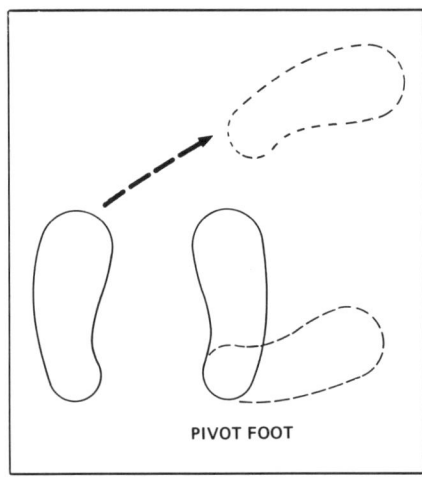

Forward Pivot.

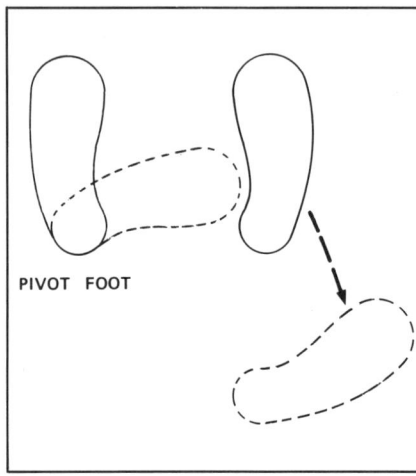

Backstep Pivot.

should finish with your hips facing a side wall. Whether you pivot and step forward or backward depends on where the ball rebounds and whether you have to move up or back to reach it. Further adjustments in body position can be made by "cross-stepping" forward or backward. During any pivot motion, your eyes must not lose contact with the ball, and your face should be directly toward the ball.

Points to Remember:

1. Decide quickly where the ball is to be hit, and pivot to that side immediately.
2. After the pivot, the body should face a sidewall.
3. Move either forward or backward to the ball by cross-stepping up or back.
4. Keep your eyes and face directed at the ball.

Forehand Stroke

The only problem remaining is to hit the ball! Forehand strokes will be discussed first, then additional information on backhand strokes will be given. The forehand stroke itself begins as the racquet is carried from the set stance through the position change that results from the pivot.

BACKSWING

As the body is turned to the side wall, so is the racquet. But the racquet continues to be pulled back so that with the elbow bent, the racquet is in a line between your body and the back wall. This is called the backswing. In this position, the racquet is held almost at right angles to the forearm, which serves to "cock" the wrist.

Completed backswing with racquet in line between the back wall and your body.

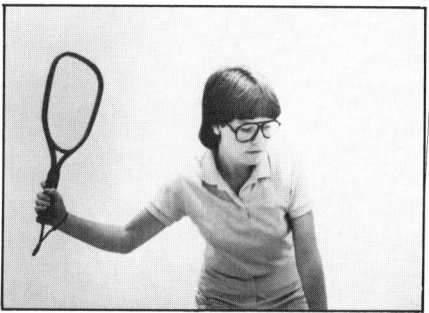

Wrist cock on the backswing.

WRIST COCK

The wrist cock is a critical part of your stroke. It is the "uncocking" or snapping of the wrist and racquet at the ball which generates the speed and power of the stroke. Without cocking the wrist, as in pulling the hammer back in a gun, there would be no way of hitting the ball with an explosive force. To be most effective, the snap or "uncocking" of the wrist must occur when the ball is contacted.

FORWARD SWING

As you prepare to swing the racquet forward, you must first shift your weight forward. This is done by stepping into the path of the ball with the foot closest to the front wall. At the same time, the forward swing of the racquet is begun by extending the elbow (i.e., straightening out the arm). It is important that during the swing, the elbow remain close to the side of the body. This position enables the ball to be contacted below waist level and prevents "over-the-shoulder" shots. Once the arm is extended, the racquet should be at the same level off the floor as your hand, with the head perpendicular to the floor, or "on edge." However, the racquet hand should lead the racquet through the swing. This position helps to maintain a "cocked" wrist through the swing.

Forward swing maintaining wrist cock.

Points to Remember:

1. On the backswing, pull the racquet back to a point directly behind you in line with your body and the back wall.
2. Hold the racquet almost at right angles to the forearm to "cock" the wrist.
3. Shift weight to your forward foot.
4. Extend the arm on the forward swing, holding the upper arm close to the body.
5. Maintain wrist cock through the swing, with the racquet head trailing the wrist and hand through the swing.
6. Keep the racquet head perpendicular to the floor and at the same level as the hand.

CONTACT

Contact with the ball should be made slightly in front of the forward foot as your weight is shifted forward. At the point of

Weight shifted forward and swinging to hit ball off of forward foot.

impact, the wrist is snapped. Contact with the ball should be made as close to the ground as possible, with your arm extended. To do this, you must bend your knees to drop your waist and racquet close to the ground.

The ball can be contacted at one of three points during its flight: (1) as it rebounds off the front wall, dropping below your waist toward the floor; (2) after the ball rebounds off the floor and bounces toward your racquet; and (3) after the ball reaches the height of its bounce and is falling back to the floor and below your waist. For experienced players, hitting the ball as it rebounds off the

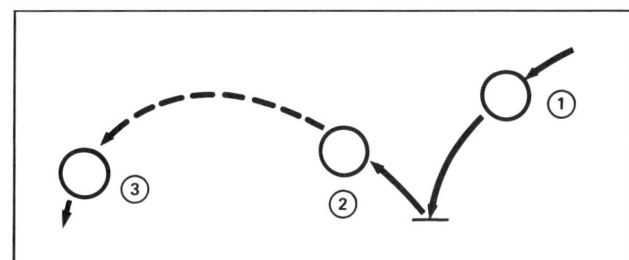

Points of contact for a rebounding ball.

floor maintains a fast tempo in the game. The beginning player, however, should wait for the ball to reach the height of its bounce and begin to rebound to the floor for the second time before hitting the ball.

Points to Remember:
1. Shift your weight onto your forward foot at the beginning of the forward swing.
2. Hit the ball slightly in front of your forward foot when it is below waist level.
3. At the point of impact, snap the wrist.
4. If possible, contact the ball low to the ground, just before it would hit the floor for the second time.

FOLLOW-THROUGH

A mistake that many beginners make is failing to complete the stroke, or to "follow through" after the hit is made. Consequently, these players "punch" at the ball with a shortened stroke and lose the force of their hit. The follow-through made after contact with the ball allows for the completion of the stroke and hitting the ball with all the force of your swing. It also allows you to recover from the stroke quickly and adjust your stance back to the set position to await your next hit.

In general, a racquetball stroke should end with the racquet swung past the midline of the body and finish in front of the forward leg. The follow-through should rotate the shoulders and

Follow-through of the forehand stroke.

hips so that they are again facing the front wall, with the back foot acting as a pivot. At the end of the stroke, your weight should be concentrated on your forward foot but balanced so that you do not fall down. During this follow-through, the body should be kept low to the ground. Standing up too quickly will cause the ball to be "carried" upward with your movement and make it difficult for you to hit low balls.

Points to Remember:
1. Follow the stroke through to the end of the swing.
2. Stay low; keep the racquet low.
3. After the ball has been contacted, allow the body to rotate toward the front wall following the direction of the arm swing.
4. Don't stand up until the follow-through is complete.

Backhand Stroke

To hit a backhand stroke, use either a backhand grip on the racquet, or turn the racquet face down by rotating the wrist. The movement begins as the forehand stroke from the set position. The pivot, however, results in the player facing the opposite side wall. Again, the pivot can be made by either stepping forward or backward, depending on the position of the ball (see page 22). After pivoting, the hips should be parallel to the side wall.

Set position before backhand.

Backhand pivot with the hips facing the side wall.

BACKSWING

The backhand stroke is begun by pulling the racquet across the body with the backswing. At the end of the backswing, the racquet is held in line between your shoulder and the back wall. In this position, the upper body must rotate more than in the forehand stroke in order for the racquet to be positioned behind the shoulder. When correctly rotated, the chin should almost rest on the shoulder of the racquet arm.

Backswing position for backhand stroke.

WRIST COCK

The racquet must be held with the wrist cocked, as in the forehand stroke. In the cocked position, the racquet is almost at a 90-degree angle to the forearm.

Wrist cock.

FORWARD SWING

As the forward swing is begun, the player's weight is shifted to the front foot. The racquet face should be held at the same level as the hand, with the racquet head trailing the hand on the forward swing to maintain the cocked position. The elbow should be held close to the body. In error, a beginning player often extends the elbow out away from the body. Consequently, power is lost, and often the ball is rebounded to the side of the court instead of forward as the racquet is pulled diagonally across the body.

Forward swing with the racquet trailing the hand.

Points to Remember:

1. Use a backhand grip, or rotate your wrist to change the position of the racquet head to hit the ball.
2. Pivot to the opposite side wall from that turned to with the forehand stroke.
3. Pull the racquet back to a position between the shoulder and the back wall.
4. Cock the wrist at the end of the backswing.
5. On the forward swing, keep your upper arm and elbow close to the body.
6. Keep the racquet head behind the hand on the forward swing.

CONTACT

To contact the ball, your weight should be forward on the front foot. Extend the elbow at the point of contact so that the racquet almost pivots around the extended arm. The racquet should contact the ball just in front of the forward foot as low to the ground as possible. When the ball is contacted, the wrist is snapped sharply to increase the impact on the ball.

Contacting the ball.

Points to Remember:

1. Your weight is shifted forward at contact with the ball.
2. Hit the ball when it is just in front of your forward foot and close to the ground.
3. At the point of contact, extend the arm, keeping the elbow close to the body.
4. As the racquet hits the ball, snap the wrist to increase the power in your stroke.

FOLLOW-THROUGH

As with the forehand, the backhand stroke is finished with a follow-through. With the follow-through, the chest and hips end up facing the front wall, and the racquet is swung to a point opposite

Follow-through.

the shoulder of the racquet arm. Without a follow-through, the strength of the swing is lost. Until the stroke is complete, keep your head down to prevent yourself from standing up before the ball leaves the racquet. Otherwise the ball will be lifted up with your movement.

Points to Remember:
1. Finish the stroke with a follow-through so that the racquet stops at a point opposite the forward shoulder.
2. Stay low after hitting the ball.

The success of either a forehand or backhand stroke is dependent upon your ability to hit the ball consistently with the same stroking motion. This means that the point of contact with the ball in relation to your body must not vary. The ony way to assure this is to MOVE on the court so that the ball is aligned properly with your stroke. Too many beginning players (and some better ones, too!) are content to hit the ball regardless of where it is, if it is within their reach. This tactic results in many unorthodox strokes in an attempt to hit the ball. Since most of these shots have never been practiced, these strokes merely rebound the ball back to the front wall rather than being accurately placed. It is the player who positions him/hersef consistently to hit the same shot who can make conscious changes in the racquet head angle or force of impact to DIRECT the ball away from the opponent's reach. Now THAT is racquetball!

Common Errors and Why You Make Them

1. I never know where the ball is going.
   A. You fail to position yourself so that the ball is contacted at the same place in relation to your body at all times. Move in the court, and go to where the ball will be. Set yourself up, and hit the ball as you have practiced.
2. I can't hit the ball hard.
   A. Check to see if you are following through rather than just "punching" at the ball and stopping your arm motion.
   B. Make sure that you are snapping your wrist at the moment of contact with the ball to increase the impact.

(Continued on page 32)

Common Errors and Why You Make Them (Cont.)

  C. Check to make sure that you are hitting the ball when it is still in front of you, i.e., off your front foot rather than behind your front foot.

3. The ball always goes "up." I can't seem to hit a low ball.
  A. Check your grip to see if the racquet head is pointed up at contact.
  B. Watch your body position to see if you are standing up before the ball leaves the racquet head. You may be "carrying" the ball up with you.
  C. Emphasize a follow-through rather than just punching at the ball.

4. I miss the ball completely, or the ball always hits a side wall.
  A. You are probably hitting the ball behind your front foot. This area is not in your field of vision, and you lose track of the ball. Hitting the ball from this position also means that your arm has not swung the racquet so that the racquet head is parallel to the front wall. Instead, the racquet head is still angled toward a side wall, causing the ball to rebound in that direction.

5. I hit the ball into the side wall.
  A. Usually this means that you have not changed from the set position to the pivot. Your hips are therefore facing the front wall rather than the side wall. As a result, your stroke comes across the body and directs the ball into the side wall.

6. I can't hit my backhand with strength and power.
  A. You are positioning yourself too close to the balls on your backhand side. You have to keep the racquet close to your body and cannot extend your arm as you swing to contact the ball with power. Also, you could be holding your elbow away from your body as you make your forward swing. This would also prevent you from extending your arm to hit the ball.

Chapter 3

Offensive Strokes

An offensive shot is designed to win a point outright by virtue of the skill with which it is hit. Regardless of where your opponent is playing, the well-executed offensive shot should always be a winner. Several basic offensive shots exist. Any offensive shot may be hit with either a forehand or backhand stroke, and the skilled player can use either stroke with equal effectiveness.

The beginning player will usually choose to hit an offensive shot from his/her forehand side. This gives credence to the observation of a player having a "weak" side, i.e., one from which an offensive shot is usually not hit (in most cases the backhand). Therefore, a good strategy to follow when playing a *"weak"-sided* opponent is to hit your offensive shots so that they must be returned with a "weak" side shot (i.e., backhand). With this strategy, if your offensive shot is not "perfect," you are usually not setting up an offensive return.

The type of offensive shot you hit is dependent upon your skill with each shot, your position on the court, and in a few instances, your opponent's court position. To hit accurate offensive shots requires hours of practice on the court. Therefore, you should not rely on offensive shots in a game situation until you can hit them consistently in practice.

Kill Shots

A kill shot is the ultimate offensive weapon of a racquetball player. By definition, a kill shot is a ball that hits the front wall so low and hard that the rebound to the floor occurs almost simultaneously with the front-wall hit. This rebound makes it virtually impossible for your opponent to return the ball even if he/she is standing in the ball's path.

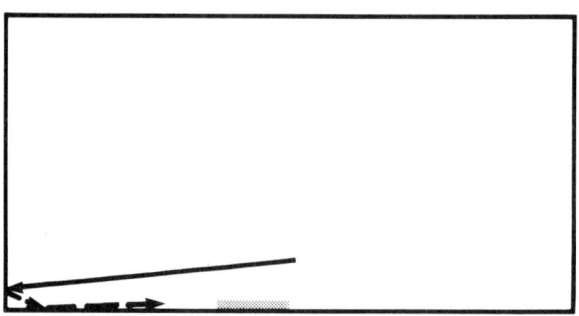

Rebound of a kill shot off the front wall.

All kill shots, except the overhead kill, should be hit when the ball is close to the floor. Contact with the ball must be made by bending your knees to drop your waist and racquet arm close to the floor. Ideally, the ball should be struck when it is positioned between your bent knee and the top of your foot. The shot is then made with

Racquet position off the court to hit a kill shot.

a normal forehand or backhand motion, with emphasis on generating power in the hit by stepping into the ball and using a good wrist snap. The harder the ball is hit, the farther away from the front

Forehand kill shot sequence.

Backhand kill shot sequence.

wall a kill shot can be successfully made. Most beginners, however, because of their weaker stroke, should concentrate on hitting kill shots from a mid court position or just behind the short line.

The critical factor in hitting a good kill shot is keeping the racquet perpendicular to the floor and the swing parallel to the floor to insure hitting a flat or level ball. A level hit will rebound off the

Racquet head perpendicular to the floor on a kill shot.

Sequence of kill shot showing racquet head perpendicular to floor.

front wall at or below the height that it hits into the wall. Thus, a low, level ball hit to the front wall has the greatest potential for achieving the desired kill shot effect.

Front Wall-Straight-In Kill Shot

A front wall-straight-in kill shot hits the front wall first and rebounds toward the back wall without touching a side wall. This shot can be hit from anyplace in the court and at anytime during play, but it is most effective if your opponent is next to (A) or behind you (B) in the court. Ideally, this kill shot should be directed toward the half of the front wall farthest away from the opposing player. Since the ball follows a straight path to the front wall, the racquet face must be parallel to this surface when it strikes the ball. In addition, keeping the swing level to the floor will insure that the ball is hit low to the front wall.

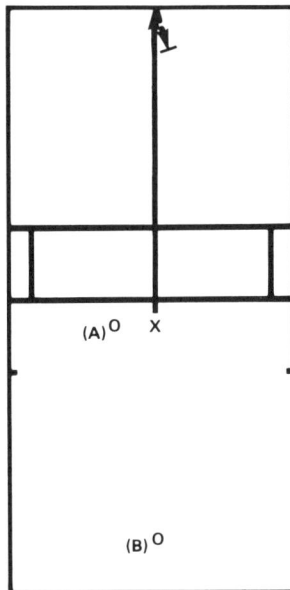

Front wall straight-in kill shot.

Front Wall-Side Wall Kill (Corner)

If the opponent is in the back court or close to a side wall, a front wall-side wall kill may be used. In this shot, the racquet is held so that the face is aimed at a corner of the front wall. As a result, the ball will hit the front wall close to the front wall-side wall crotch and quickly rebound to the nearest side wall. Depending upon the angle with which the ball is hit, the ball may bounce toward a front-or mid-court position. The success of this shot depends on

Racquethead angled to front corner for kill shot.

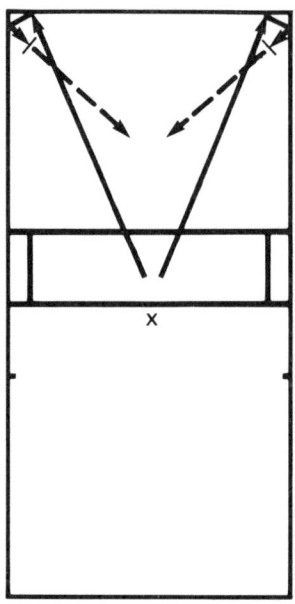

Front wall - Side wall kill (corner).

your opponent's court position and how accurately you can hit the ball. If the ball is not hit low as a kill shot should be, or if the opponent is not far enough in the back court or is toward a side wall, the shot will be a setup for an easy return to the front wall. One way to adjust for a quick-reacting opponent who covers the court well is to hit the corner kill at a sharper angle so that the ball rebounds toward the front-court position.

Side Wall-Front Wall (Pinch Kill)

The pinch kill shot hits one side wall before rebounding into the front wall. An advantage of hitting the pinch kill rather than the corner kill is simply the placement of the rebounding ball. Where the corner kill is more likely to rebound close to a mid-court position, the pinch kill rebounds tightly into a front corner. However, to be most effective with the pinch kill, the opponent should be next to or behind you in the court. Whether the shot is directed to the left or right front corner depends partly on your position in the court, but more importantly on your opponent's position. Ideally, you should always hit the ball so that the rebound off the front wall is traveling away from the opponent. If this can't be done, then at least hit the ball so that it rebounds toward the opponent's

Offensive Strokes 39

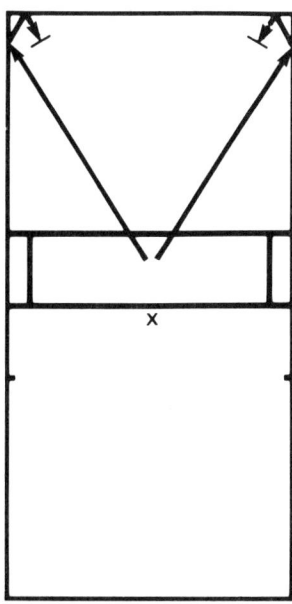

Side wall - Front wall kill (pinch).

weak side. A shot to the weak side, even if not perfectly hit, should not result in an offensive return.

To hit a pinch kill (as with the corner kill), the racquet face upon contact with the ball must be angled to the side wall rather than

Pinch kill away from opponent.

held parallel to the front wall. The ball must be contacted close to the ground. To do this, bend your knees, drop your waist, and extend your racquet arm down. In all other respects, the technique for hitting this kill shot is similar to that for a forehand or backhand stroke.

The pinch kill is ideal for the beginning player because he/she can make a mistake in hitting this shot and still score a point. Since the rebound is to a front-court position, even a ball hit too high or one that rebounds off the floor may be impossible for your opponent to reach as long as he/she is in the back court.

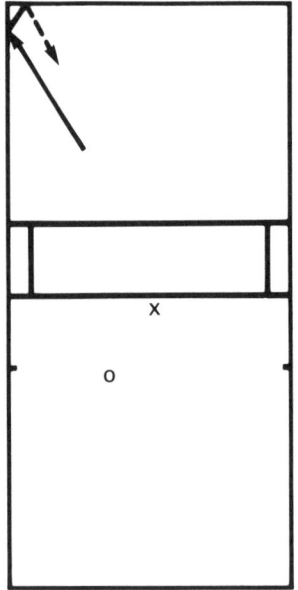

Pinch kill hit away from opponent.

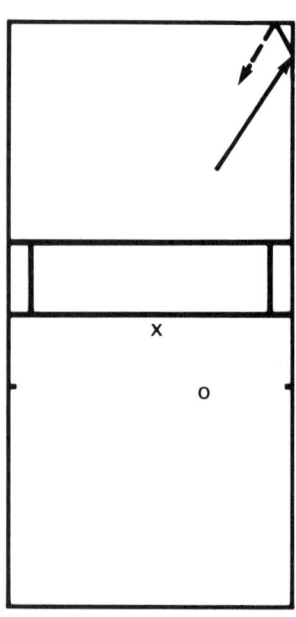

Pinch kill hit to opponent's backhand.

Overhead Kill

The overhead kill shot is popular with beginning players but falls out of favor as the player develops other offensive weapons. The object of the overhead kill is the same as for any kill shot, but the stroking technique is different. This kill shot is hit off a ball that is above shoulder level rather than close to the ground. It is hit from the forehand side with much the same motion used in a tennis serve. The stroke is begun by pivoting and pulling the racquet back as if to hit a forehand stroke (see page 22). However, as the foreward swing is begun, the racquet is lifted in a circular motion as if you were going to throw it to the front wall. The chest and hips are rotated to face the front wall as you step forward to hit the ball. The ball is contacted just in front of the forward foot with an extended arm. At contact, the face of the racquet should be parallel to the front wall. To assume this position, a Western grip is preferred over any other forehand grip to turn the face of the racquet. To maximize the power of the stroke, the ball should always be hit with the arm in an extended position and the stroke completed with a follow-through, dropping the racquet across the body. Ideally, the ball should be directed low into a front corner of

Sequence of overhead kill shot.

the court. To have the best chance of success, the overhead kill should hit a side wall as well as the front wall to deaden the rebound of the ball. Otherwise, if not hit perfectly, the ball will rebound high into the air at the same angle at which it hit the wall. The high bounce gives even a slow opponent adequate time to position him/herself for the return. Consequently, the overhead kill is considered a "low-percentage" shot because it is hard to score a point off a ball that is not hit perfectly. Therefore, beginning players are advised to be patient and wait for the ball to drop below waist level. Then, a corner or pinch kill can be hit. Both of these kill shots are more difficult to return than the overhead kill, even if all shots are hit incorrectly.

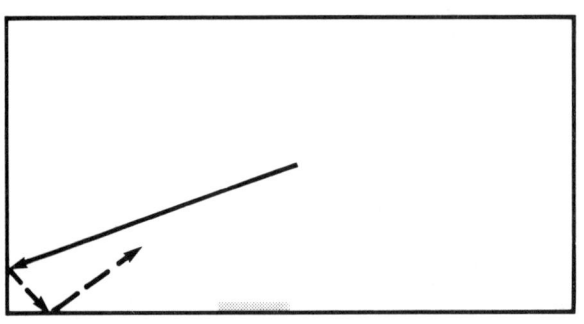

Rebound of overhead kill bouncing high off the floor.

Points to Remember:
1. To be effective, kill shots should combine a low ball hit to the front wall with a forceful stroke and sharp wrist snap.
2. To hit a good kill shot, wait for the ball to fall low to the ground — at least below your knee.
3. When hitting a kill shot, bend your knees and drop your waist to lower your racquet arm to the ground.
4. To hit a level kill shot, keep your racquet face perpendicular to the floor, and swing level with the floor.
5. To direct a kill shot to a front corner, you must angle your racquet face to the corner that you wish to hit.
6. Always angle your kill shot away from your opponent's court position to insure a successful shot.

Passing Shots

A passing shot, unlike the kill shot, requires no new techniques to master. Its effectiveness depends only on your opponent's court position and your ability to place the ball. The passing shot, as its name implies, is a ball that literally goes "past" the opponent.

Therefore, it is most advantageous when the opposing player is in the front-, mid-, or center-court areas. In this way, the ball can go "past" the opponent and "beat" him/her into the back court. If hit

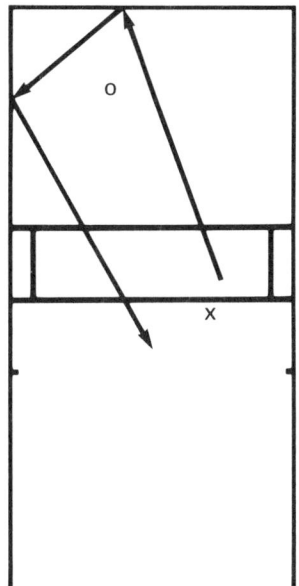

Passing shot hit to opponent in front court.

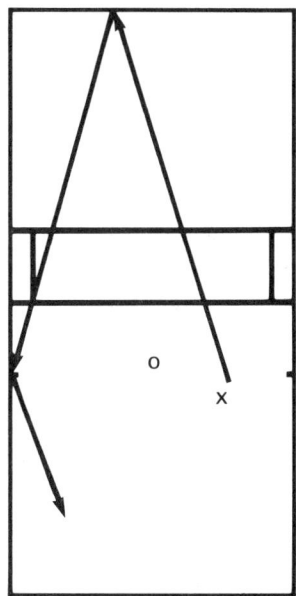

Passing shot hit to opponent in center court.

low off the front wall, a passing shot will die in the back court and not rebound into a center-court position. Without rebounding hard off the back wall, the ball in essence is "out-of-play" except to a heroic effort. At the very least, if the ball is returned, it will usually be a desperation shot that you can return for a winner or at least will push your opponent to use up his/her energy reserves.

The most critical error made by beginning players when using a passing shot is hitting the ball with too much force. As a result, instead of dying in the back court, the ball rebounds off the back wall into play and negates the advantage that the passing shot offers.

The passing shot can be hit with either a forehand, backhand, or overhead stroke. The ball should be directed to hit the front wall at a point between waist and knee height off the floor. In all cases, however, the lower the rebound off the front wall, the less chance that a return will be made. The ball can either be hit directly to a back corner or angled to rebound from the front wall to contact a side wall on the way to the back court. If the ball is angled toward a side wall, it should hit either at the same distance or farther from the front wall as your opponent is standing. This will help not only

Passing shot using the side wall.

to slow the movement of the ball into the back court but discourage your opponent from trying to hit the ball as it rebounds off the front wall because it will be out of reach. Should the ball hit the side wall in front of your opponent's court position, it will pass through the center court and allow your opponent to make a return shot.

Two types of passing shots are common — the down-the-line pass and the cross-court pass.

Down-The-Line Pass

The down-the-line pass could really be called the down-the-wall (wallpaper) pass. This ball is hit so that it travels in a line along the side wall, 1 to 3 feet from it and below waist level. As stated before, hitting the ball too hard will cause a strong rebound off the

Down-the-line pass.

back wall and possibly allow a return to be made. This passing shot is ideally hit when you are between your opponent and the side wall down which you are hitting or when the opposing player is "caught" in a front-court position. In either case, hit the ball toward the side wall that is the farthest distance from your opponent. If he/she is playing a center-court position, hit to the backhand side. A forehand stroke should be used to hit passing shots to the forehand side of the court and a backhand stroke for balls directed to the backhand side.

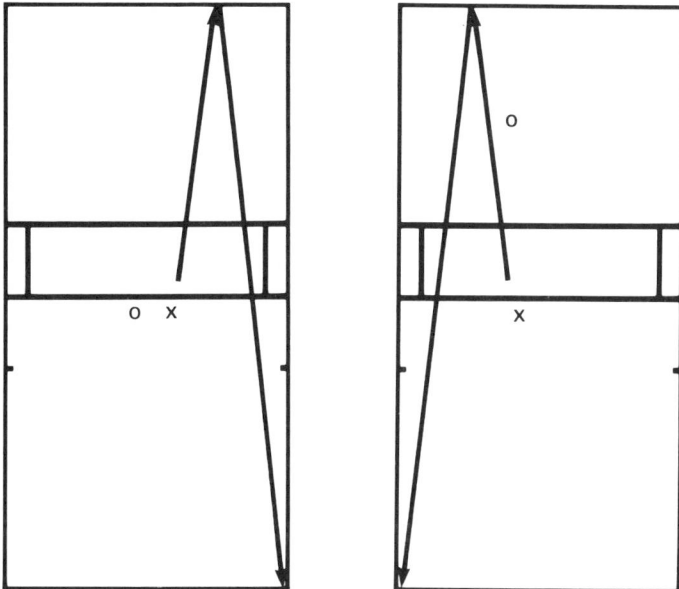

Cross-court passing shot.

Cross-Court Pass

The cross-court pass moves the ball from one side of the court to the other in order to "pass" the opponent. It does this by following the path of a "V" across the court. Dependent upon where you are positioned in the court, the ball will rebound off the front wall close to its center. You must experiment with the exact placement of the ball as you hit from different court positions. What will always be true is that the ball will rebound from the front wall at an angle equal to the angle of impact. To prevent the opponent from hitting the rebound off the front wall, this angle must be large enough to avoid the opponent's reach.

As with a down-the-line pass, the cross-court shot may be hit with a forehand, backhand, or overhead stroke. It is ideally used when your opponent is on your side of the court, is in a center-court position, or is positioned closer to the front wall. One advantage of the passing shot is that it can be hit from anyplace on the court, including the back court, since the success of the shot depends more on your opponent's court position. It is an easy shot to learn and win with because most right-handed players can use their stronger forehands to hit cross-court passing shots to their opponent's weaker backhands.

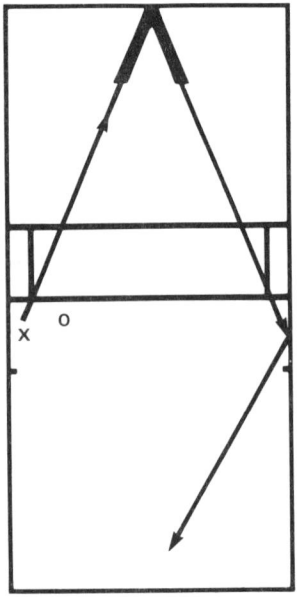

Cross court passing shot with opponent close to side wall.

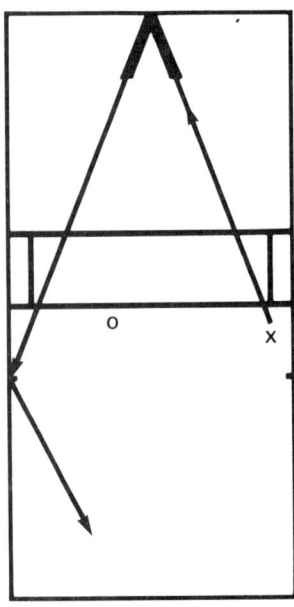

Cross court passing shot with opponent in center court.

As with a down-the-line pass, a ball that rebounds low into the back court has the greatest chance of success. This ball may also hit a side wall before rebounding into the back-court area. As stated earlier, however, care must be taken to insure that the ball does not rebound through a center-court position or in front of the opponent. Hitting a side wall will also help to slow the speed of the ball on the court, allowing you to hit the ball with more force and still have a successful passing shot.

Since a wide margin of error exists with how hard and at what angle the ball should be hit, successful cross-court passing shots can be made by even the most beginning player.

Points to Remember:

1. A passing shot can be hit with any stroke. Its success is dependent upon your opponent's court position.
2. Do not use a passing shot when your opponent is in a back-court position.
3. A passing shot can be hit cross-court or down-the-line from anyplace on the court.
4. The lower the passing shot rebounds off the front wall, the greater its chance of being a winning shot.
5. The passing shot may hit a side wall after rebounding from the front wall, but it should not be angled to hit in front of the opponent or through the center-court area.
6. Hitting the passing shot too hard will cause the ball to rebound off the back wall into play.

Common Errors and How to Correct Them

1. My kill shots always hit the floor before they reach the front wall.
   A. Usually you have angled the racquet face down at the point of impact with the ball, thus driving the ball into the ground. Concentrate on keeping your racquet face perpendicular to the floor and the stroke parallel to the floor.
2. My kill shots are never low enough to the front wall.
   A. Be patient and wait for the ball to drop closer to the ground before hitting it. This means that you will have to bend your knees and lower your waist to drop your racquet to the ball. Try to make contact with the ball just off the tops of your shoes. If this does not help, you may be scooping at the ball with the racquet and hitting it on the upswing, which lifts the ball to the front wall higher than you want it to hit. A level swing with the floor will correct this problem.
3. I hit my cross-court shots right back to my opponent because the ball bounces off a side wall into the center court.
   A. Take some angle off your hit and aim more for the center of the front wall.

Common Errors and How to Correct Them (Cont.)

4. My down-the-line passing shot always hits the side wall.

    A. Your racquet head is not parallel to the front wall when you contact the ball, but is angled toward the side wall that you are hitting. Hold the wrist stiff and swing through the ball. Also, check to make sure that you are contacting the ball off your forward foot. Contacting the ball in front of or behind this position will cause the ball to rebound at an angle off the front wall.

5. My overhead kill shot hits (a) the floor first or (b) too high off the front wall.

    A. (a) When the floor is hit first, either the ball is hit when it is too far in front of you or when your wrist is bent too much, causing the racquet head to be angled to the floor. Check the position of your body relative to the ball when you hit the overhead, and hold the racquet so that it appears to be an extension of your arm.

    (b) Hitting the ball too high off the front wall usually results from hitting the ball too far behind your front foot or even over your head, which prohibits you from angling the hit downward. Again, check the position of the ball when you make contact, and be sure that the contact point is in front of your forward foot.

6. My passing shots always rebound off the back wall into a center-court position.

    A. Take some of the force off your stroke, and hit the ball lower off the front wall to insure a shorter rebound from the back. If this does not help, try to hit a side wall to deaden the ball's movement.

Chapter Four

Defensive Strokes

Rather than scoring a point, the purpose of a defensive shot is to PREVENT your opponent from hitting a winning shot. This goal can be achieved only if your shot is too high, preventing a kill-shot return, or rebounds to a court position that provides little space from which to hit an offensive return. Ideally, the best defensive shot is hit in such a way as to have the ball rebound from the front wall high into the back court and close to the side wall. Several strokes accomplish this purpose, at least one of which should immediately be in your repertoire of shots.

Ceiling Shot (Front Wall-Ceiling)

This ceiling shot can be hit with a forehand or backhand stroke off a ball that falls below waist level or with an overhead stroke on a high ball. A front-wall-to-ceiling shot hits the front wall before the ceiling. Upon contact with the front wall, the ball rebounds to the ceiling close to the front wall-ceiling crotch and then is directed downward to bounce on the floor just past the short line. If hit with enough force, the rebound of the ball off the floor will carry the ball high over the head of the opponent and into a back corner, dying upon impact with the back corner. Since the ball must be returned before striking the floor twice, your opponent must hit the ball

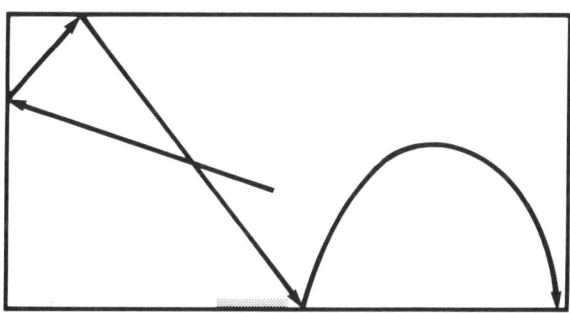

Front wall - Ceiling shot.

from this corner position without the benefit of a rebound off the back wall or floor. Thus, this court position makes it difficult to hit an offensive shot because of the ball's proximity to the walls. However, the harder you hit a front wall-ceiling shot, the higher the height of the bounce off the floor and the greater the chance the ball will hit and rebound off the back wall. Therefore, care must be taken to hit the ball with enough force to provide a bounce high enough to force the opponent to the back corner but not so high as to cause a rebound off the back wall into a center-court position.

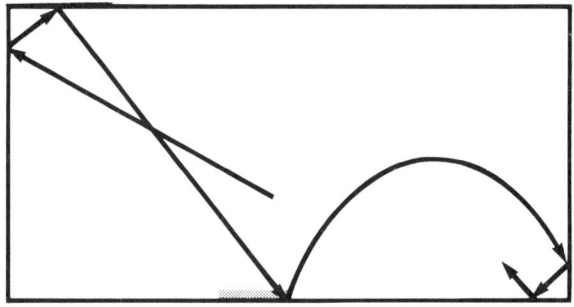

Front wall - Ceiling hit with too much force and rebounding off the back wall.

The front wall-ceiling shot hit from a ball that has dropped below waist level begins as any other forehand or backhand stroke. The pivot to the side wall is followed by the backswing with the wrist cocked. However, as the forward swing is begun, the racquet head must be turned back, or "opened," toward the ceiling. This

Open racquet for ceiling shot.

racquet face position directs the ball toward the top of the front wall. In addition, the use of a pendulum, or "scooping" swing, instead of a stroke that is parallel to the floor, will help to "lift" the ball to the height needed.

Pendulum swing.

The front wall-ceiling shot hit with an overhead stroke, whether from the forehand or backhand side, is similar in technique to an overhead kill shot (see page 40). Like the kill shot, contact with the ball is made just off the forward foot, with the hips and chest facing the front wall and the arm extended. A Western grip is preferred by many players, since it opens the face of the racquet to the ceiling. The difference between the ceiling shot and the offensive kill return is the angle of the racquet face when the ball is

Backhand overhead ceiling shot (continued on page 52)

contacted. The face must be angled toward the top of the front wall. To do this, the wrist cannot be snapped from its laid-back position on the forward swing. This will keep the racquet directed upward. The stroke should finish with a follow-through to insure hitting the ball with power.

Laid back racquet for overhead ceiling shot.

A front wall-ceiling shot is most effective if hit when your opponent is already in the back court. The ball strikes the floor close to the short line, which means that if your opponent is playing nearby, he/she may be tempted to hit the ball immediately after the bounce. A back-court position would not result in the same temptation, and the desired effect of the ceiling shot can be achieved.

To insure the most difficult return possible, the front wall-ceiling shot should be directed to "run" along a side wall before it bounces into the back corner. If in addition the ball is directed to your opponent's backhand side, this defensive shot may not only result in a weak return but possibly no return at all. Thus, this defensive shot may actually score a point for you.

Ceiling Shot (Ceiling-Front Wall Shot)

A variation of the front wall-ceiling shot is one that hits both walls but in the reverse order. Although both ceiling shots are hit with a similar technique, this ceiling shot is hit with a racquet that is angled more toward the ceiling. The ball should be directed to hit the ceiling approximately 2 to 3 feet from the ceiling/front wall crotch. With this stroke, the ball will rebound to the floor, hitting in front of the service zone before bouncing into the back-court area.

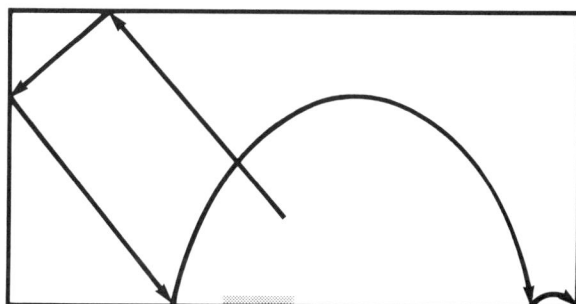

Ceiling - front wall defensive shot.

The advantage of a ceiling-front wall shot is that it can be an effective defensive shot even if your opponent is near center court. The ball rebounds to the floor in front of the service line, which means that your opponent must retreat to the back court to await the fall of the ball. Thus, with this shot the opponent will be forced into a poor court position. In all other respects, the strategic use of a ceiling-front wall shot is the same as for a front wall-ceiling shot: (1) keep the ball in play; (2) move your opponent to a back-court position; and (3) force a return that is not an offensive shot.

Either ceiling shot can be hit from any part of the court and should be practiced from all court positions. If you are standing to one side of center, you can hit the shot down the closest side wall (wallpaper shot) or hit cross-court to the opposite corner. The cross-court ceiling shot requires more power in the stroke because of the diagonal court distance to be covered as well as the need for accurate placement. If the ball is not hit at a sharp angle, the rebound forward will be away from the side wall and will provide for easy stroking room. A similar problem exists with a ceiling shot hit down-the-line if it does not "hug" the wall. Thus, although the ceiling shot is one of the easiest defensive strokes to learn, unless time is taken to practice placement, the true advantage of the shot cannot be achieved.

Points to Remember:
1. When the ball hits the racquet, the angle of the racquet head must be directed to the spot on the front wall or ceiling that you want the ball to hit.
2. To hit a ceiling shot from a ball below waist level, open the racquet face and use a pendulum swing.
3. Ceiling shots hit with an overhead stroke should contact the ball in front of the forward foot with an extended arm.
4. Angle all ceiling shots so that they rebound into a back corner, preferably to your opponent's backhand.
5. Hitting a ceiling shot with too much force can result in the ball rebounding off the back wall and into play.

Lob Shot

A lob shot is not played as often in competitive racquetball as other defensive shots. This is due to the popularity of the composite/graphite racquets and the use of pressurized balls. The lob is a shot that requires finesse and placement, not the power and strength for which this equipment was designed. Therefore, players that choose a fast-moving, power game often do not have the finesse necessary to hit a lob return.

A lob is struck with a technique similar to a ceiling shot hit from a ball falling below waist level. Both shots, whether hit with a forehand or backhand stroke, require a pendulum forward swing. Contact with the ball should be made with an extended arm and open face racquet off the forward foot. Although not much force is required to hit this ball properly, the ball should be struck with your weight shifted toward the front wall. Finish the stroke with a follow-through high over your head. This arm motion and the racquet face angle serve to "lift" the ball.

Like the ceiling shot, the lob is returned high to the front wall, approximately 6 to 8 feet from the ceiling. However, the lob shot

Backhand lob shot.

differs from the ceiling shot in that the ball never rebounds to touch the ceiling. Rather, the ball slowly moves along a line close to the ceiling and high over center court, falling "dead" into a back corner with little or no rebound from the back wall. When perfectly hit, the slow movement of this ball allows you time to reposition yourself on the court, yet forces your opponent into the disadvantages of a back-corner return.

Similar to the ceiling shot, a lob may be hit down-the-line or cross-court. If the lob is hit down-the-line, it is preferable to use a backhand shot down the left side wall and a forehand shot to the right side wall for more control. A cross-court lob may be hit with

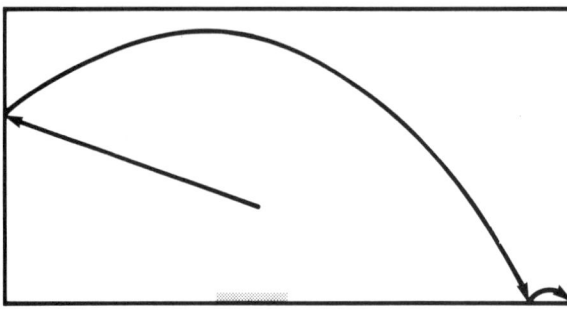

Lob defensive shot.

either stroke. The purpose of both shots is to place the ball in a back-court position to prevent an offensive return. Thus, the lob presents many of the same problems to your opponent as the ceiling shot does. The reason why it is not hit more often is because it is a difficult shot to hit correctly. Since the ball does not rebound from the ceiling on the way to the back court, the ball, if hit too hard, will merely rebound off the back wall into a center-court position. Thus,

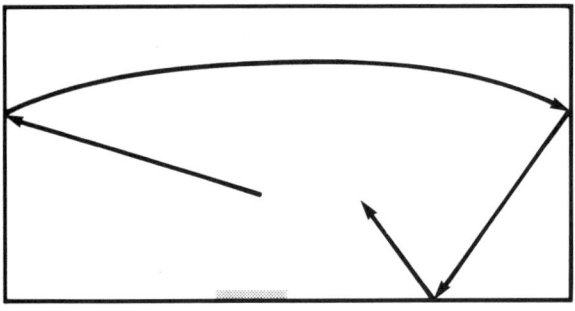

Lob shot rebounding into center court off the back wall.

the advantage of a back-corner placement is lost. In addition, because the ball moves so slowly, it is easy to hit a strong return unless the lob is placed correctly. To minimize any possible rebound off the back wall, aim the lob so that the ball just brushes against a side wall. This "meeting" will slow the ball and deaden its fall to the floor. For most beginners, the finesse with which this ball must be hit is hard to manage in a game situation where quick movements are necessary. Yet, the lob does offer an interesting variation for the player who can use it, including changing the pace of the game.

Points to Remember:

1. Remember to pivot the hips and use a pendulum swing with an open racquet face to hit the ball.

2. Hit the ball as hard as you think necessary, then take some force off your swing.
3. Finish the stroke with a follow-through, with the racquet ending up high over your shoulder.
4. To take some power out of your shot, aim the ball to "brush" the side wall close to the back corner.
5. To be more effective, lob only to a back corner.

High Z-Ball or Three-Wall Shot

Like the other defensive shots, the high Z or three-wall shot is designed to move the opponent into a back corner. The high Z can be hit with either an overhead stroke from a high ball or a stroke using a pendulum motion on a waist-level return. To insure proper placement of the ball, the racquet head at contact must again be angled in the direction toward which the ball should travel. This means that the racquet face should be slightly open. In all other respects, the high Z stroke also resembles one of the other defensive shots. The overhead stroke is similar to the overhead ceiling shot (see page 52), while the high Z, hit from a waist-level ball, is similar to the lob (see page 54).

As in other defensive shots, the high Z must be directed to hit high off the front wall and close to a ceiling crotch (3 to 4 feet from it). However, a high Z differs from other defensive shots in that the ball moves diagonally across the court to the back wall. In essence, the movement of the ball describes a "Z" through the court. To follow this path, the ball must hit the front wall not only high, but within 3 to 4 feet of a front corner crotch. After contact with the front wall, the ball hits the closest side wall and rebounds to follow the long diagonal of the court to a back corner position, hitting the back wall and completing the path of the "Z".

The placement of the ball on the front wall is critical to the effectiveness of this shot. If hit too low, the Z ball is an easy setup for your opponent. This is because the ball passes over a center-court position when following the diagonal. A ball hit too low will pass through the center court area within arm's reach of your opponent. As long as the ball is hit high off the front wall, it will pass high over the center court and force your opponent into a back-court position to return the ball.

Depending upon the strength of the hit, the Z ball may or may not hit a second side wall before falling into the back corner. If hit

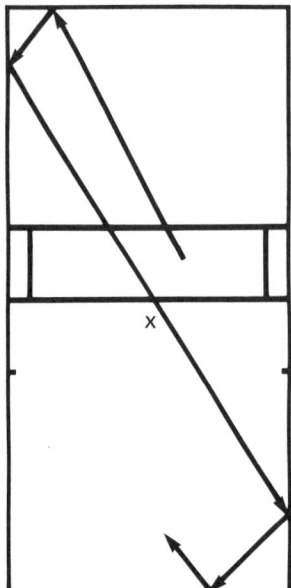 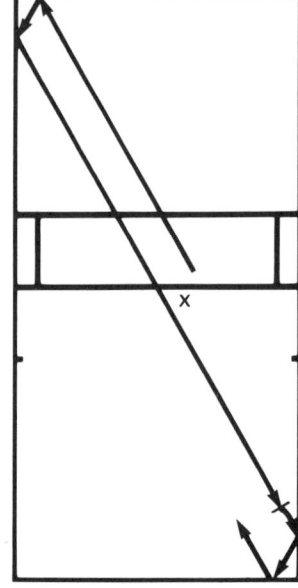

High Z "three wall" defensive shot.   *High Z defensive shot hitting floor before back corner.*

hard, a second wall will be hit on the opposite side from the first. Thus, the name "three"-wall is often used to identify this shot. In this situation, the ball will "run the corner" before touching the floor by hitting the side wall, the back wall, and then the floor in succession.

Because the ball "covers" so much of the court on a Z-ball return, women and beginning level playes often do not have a powerful enough stroke to hit the shot well. It is good to practice this shot often and feel confident about hitting it before trying a Z-ball return in a game situation.

Although a Z ball may be hit from anywhere in the court, you should try it from a center-court position if your shot is weak. Stronger players will be effective with a high Z hit even from the back court. Because of the path followed by the ball, the Z is best hit to the opposite corner from your court position. Otherwise, the angle off the front wall will not be great enough to cause a rebound along the diagonal.

The Z-ball or three-wall shot is very effective in causing a weak return, especially if the ball "runs the corner." In the back corner, there is little room to place a racquet and stroke through the ball unless timing is perfect and a good wrist snap is used. Therefore, this shot is often hit by more experienced players not only to force a bad court position on the opponent, but to "handcuff" him/her as well.

Points to Remember:

1. Hit the ball high off the front wall and close to the side wall/front wall crotch.
2. Use a stroke similar to an overhead ceiling shot for balls over your shoulder and a lob return for waist-high balls.
3. Hit the ball hard enough to "run the corner" of the back court.
4. Hit the high Z to the corner opposite from the side of the court in which you are positioned.

Around-the-Wall Ball

The around-the-wall ball is a defensive shot that hits three walls before touching the floor. It differs from the high Z shot in that the ball is first hit high to a side wall. The ball then rebounds to the front wall and finally to the opposite side wall from the initial hit. The closer to the front wall-side wall crotch the ball is aimed, the farther back on the opposite side wall the ball will rebound. Since the purpose of this shot, like other defensive shots, is to force the opponent into a back-court position, hitting close to a front corner

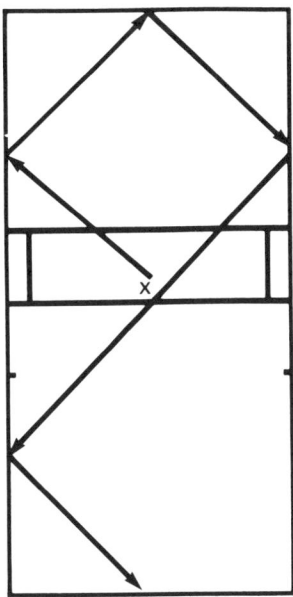

Around-the-wall shot.

is advised. If the ball strikes the first side wall too far from the front, the rebound will merely follow a path back to a center-court position.

The stroke used to hit an around-the-wall ball is the same as for the high Z. This shot must be practiced, however, to insure that the proper racquet angle is used to hit the ball close to the front corner. Although not used often, the around-the-wall shot is probably most effective against a beginning player who has difficulty determining the rebound angle of the ball or against any player to change the pace of the game.

Points to Remember:

1. Hit the around-the-wall ball with the same technique used for a high-Z ball.
2. Angle the ball close to the front wall-side wall crotch for the most effective hit.
3. Although not used often, this ball may be effective against beginning players and as a change-of-pace ball.

Common Errors and How to Correct Them

1. My ceiling shots never hit the ceiling.
   A. If the ball is hit from a position below the waist, you are not "scooping" or hitting underneath the ball to lift it high enough to hit the front wall and/or ceiling. If you are using an overhead stroke, the ball is probably too far in front of you when you contact it, or your racquet head is not angled toward the ceiling to direct the ball upward.
2. My ceiling shots hit the ceiling straight over my head.
   A. For both waist-level and overhead shots, you have angled your racquet too much, and the racquet face is almost parallel to the ceiling. In addition, with the overhead stroke, the ball is probably contacted over your head rather than in front of your forward foot.
3. My ceiling shots rebound off the back wall into the playing area.
   A. You are hitting the ball too hard or with too little angle off the front wall. Aim closer to the front wall-ceiling crotch, and ease the force of your stroke.
4. My lob always hits the ceiling.
   A. You have too much force in your hit and/or too much angle on the racquet head. Hit the ball softer, and aim for a point lower on the front wall.
5. My lob always hits the back wall and rebounds to center court.
   A. Try to angle the hit more into the back corner of the court, then limit the force with which the ball is hit. If the ball does rebound into the court, it will at least be along the wall and will still provide little stroking room.
6. My high Z does not hit the back wall corner but goes straight into the back wall.
   A. Angle your hit into the front wall closer to the front wall-side wall crotch by changing the direction of the racquet head.
7. My high Z bounces too high off the back wall and gives my opponent an easy return.
   A. Hit the ball lower to the front wall, or softer and with more of an upward stroking motion so that the ball arches into the back court.
8. My high Z ball always rebounds off the front wall-side wall and bounces at center court, where it is returned by my opponent.
   A. Make sure that you are pivoting your hips before you stroke and that you are stepping into the ball. If you rely only on the

(Continued on page 62)

Common Errors and How to Correct Them (Cont.)

strength of your arm to hit the ball, the force may not be great enough and the ball may not complete the diagonal of the court before touching the court floor.

9. My around-the-wall ball rebounds into a center position.
    A. Hit the ball with the racquet angled closer to a front-wall corner. This will cause the ball to rebound deeper into the back court.
10. My around-the-wall ball hits the floor before it hits the second side wall.
    A. You need to hit the ball harder and/or aim it to rebound higher off the first side wall so that the ball will carry through to the back court before touching the floor.

Chapter Five

Serves in Racquetball

Serving is the most important offensive weapon in the arsenal of a beginning player. For the intermediate player, the serve either "sets" up a winning shot or prevents the opponent from scoring on the return of serve. The effectiveness of the serve is due to the controlled way in which it can be hit. This is the only time when contact with the ball is made at a predetermined location. Thus, you can play to your strengths and your opponent's weaknesses if you can consistently serve your best shot.

There are only five basic serves. Each serve, however, can be changed to give a slightly different look by varying the power with which it is hit, its height of rebound off the front wall, and the angle of rebound into the back court. With these variations, the basic serves can become hundreds of different shots. The wise player mixes these variations to keep his/her opponent guessing as to "where" the next ball will be served. However, the serve chosen should only be hit after thought is given to an opponent's strengths and skills. Even a well-placed serve, if hit so that an opponent can return it with his/her favorite shot, is nothing more than a nice "setup." Similarly, a good player never hits a weak serve merely for the sake of variety if he/she is not sure that an equally weak return will follow.

For an oponent who you have never seen play, a good strategy is simply to serve to his/her backhand with your best serve. If a player has a weakness, it is usually on the backhand side, and at least this strategy will increase the odds of your winning the point with your serve.

Most important, in order to make these variations effective, your serve must not become predictable, either in the position that you take in the service court or in the technique with which you strike the ball. Ideally, all serves should be hit from a similar position on the court, with a similar stroke. Usually a center-court position and normal forehand stroke are used. In this way, it is difficult, if

Serving position on the court.

not impossible, for your opponent to anticipate the positioning of your serve. This means that variation in your serve must be a result of the amount of wrist snap or the position of the racquet face at the moment of contact with the ball. Either factor will affect the angle of hit or the power of the stroke.

Since you as the server are the only one who knows where the serve will be hit, you should also anticipate the placement of the returned ball. So take the time before each serve to not only plan the best serve, but the most likely return and how best to play the ball. Ideally, if the serve is not an outright winner, at least a poor return should occur, setting you up for your best offensive stroke.

The serve provides the server with the offensive advantage in the game. To serve without purpose or thought to your opponent's skill gives up this advantage and possibly the serve with it.

Legal Serves

For a serve to be legal, a ball is hit after rebounding off the floor within the service zone. After the racquet is contacted, the ball must strike the front wall before any other part of the court. However, the rebound from the front wall may touch one side wall before the ball falls to the floor behind the short line. The ball may not touch the floor in front of the short line. Neither the ceiling nor the back wall can be hit before the ball reaches the floor.

Most serves are hit with a forehand stroke. The server stands as far back as possible in the service zone with his/her hips pivoted to the side wall. Ideally, both feet should be placed along the short line. This provides as much service zone as possible in which to step forward when contacting the ball. Stepping out of the service zone during the serve is illegal.

To begin the serve, the ball rolls off the fingertips of the open hand and is dropped to the floor. The arm should be extended to the front wall so that the ball is dropped as far forward in the service zone as possible. If the ball is not dropped close to the service line,

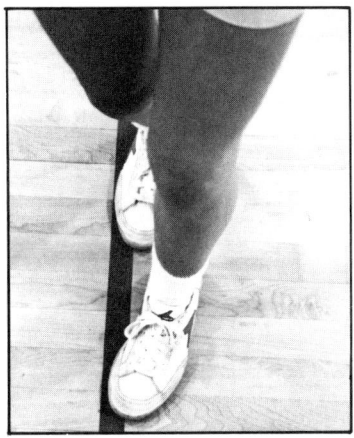

Foot placement to begin serve.

Ball drop for service.

the server will move past the ball when stepping forward to hit it. Thus, contact with the ball will occur behind the forward foot, and much of the force of the stroke will be lost.

At the beginning of the serve, the racquet has already completed the backswing and is held perpendicular to the back wall. When the ball leaves the hand, the forward swing of the racquet begins. The type of swing used (level or pendulum) and the height of the ball off the floor at contact are dependent upon the serve being hit. In any serve, however, it is essential to step into the stroke. The shifting of the body's weight from the back of the service zone to the foot that steps toward the service line provides additional power.

The serve, as any other stroke, is completed with a follow-through, the final position of the racquet being dependent upon the type of serve used. It is important to always hit "through" the ball rather than merely "punch" at it if a strong serve is desired.

Although most serves are hit with a forehand stroke, on occasion a backhand or overhead stroke may be used.

The following five serves are designed to follow the rules of service as well as place the opponent in a poor court position from which to hit an offensive return. As described with defensive strokes, this means hitting a ball into a back corner of the court. On all serves, it is important to keep the ball in the back corners and away from the midline of the court. A return from the middle of the court provides too many opportunities for offensive shots and prevents the server from holding a center-court position. Thus, the following serves should be directed wide of the midline of the court and should only rebound back to a center-court position after bouncing twice on the floor and being ruled a dead ball!

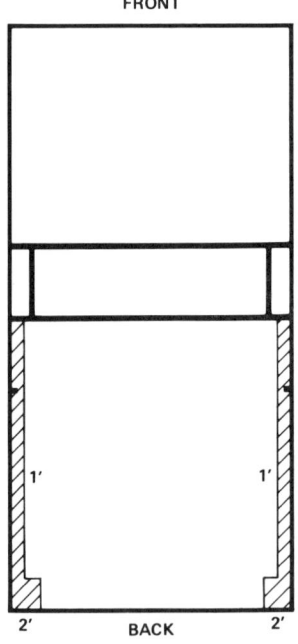

Court areas for served ball to be directed.

Lob

The lob serve is hit identically to the lob defensive shot, with the ball following the same path through the court (see page 56). The serve may be hit cross-court or down-the-line. As in the defensive lob, the ball must be hit high to the front wall, and the rebound should arch its way high over center court to die in a back-court corner. To do this, the forward swing of the stroke must involve a pendulum motion, with the racquet face slightly open to the ceiling. The ball is hit below waist level and lifted to the point of contact with the front wall. The stroke is finished with the racquet held high over the forward shoulder. As in the defensive lob, a lob serve requires finesse rather than power.

Lob Serve.

To insure that the ball will die in the back court, the lob serve can graze a side wall close to the back wall. This rebound will slow the movement of the ball. As a result, the serve must be accurately directed to a corner. Accuracy in placement is critical. If the ball does not "handcuff" your opponent in the back corner, this slow-moving ball will be an easy setup for an offensive return. If this is difficult for you to do, hit the serve to the opponent's backhand. This will provide for a margin of error in placement because it will force a weak-side return.

To increase the accuracy of the lob serve to the backhand side of the court, many players will change their center-court serving position and move to that side of the service zone. In addition, they will hit the ball with a backhand stroke using the same pendulum swing and open racquet face as on the forehand side. Although there is little deception in this maneuver, the difficulty in returning a lob serve comes not in surprising the opponent as much as in placing the ball. This court position allows for better placement because the ball is not hit at an angle. Rather, the racquet head is parallel to the front wall and the ball is hit straight.

The lob is a good serve to use to change the pace of the game and to slow down a fast-moving opponent who likes to return serves hard to the front wall. The lob can be varied by hitting the serve at a "half lob" position, i.e., one which is about shoulder height at the peak of its arch. Again, accuracy of placement is critical in the success of this serve.

Drive Serve

A drive serve is hit with a strong forehand stroke, as it is the hardest serve hit. To maximize the power in the stroke, it is essential that you turn your hips sideways to the front wall and that you meet the ball by stepping into it during the forward swing. The ball should be contacted low in relation to the body — somewhere between the bent knee and the ankle. The forward swing should be level to the ground and the ball met just in front of the forward foot. The follow-through should be low to the ground and should pull the shoulders around to finish the stroke facing the front wall. This serve resembles the kill shot in technique.

To be most effective, the drive serve should be hit low to the front wall to insure a low ball rebounding into the back court. Keeping the ball low adds to the difficulty in the return.

There is not one particular area of the court to which the drive serve should be directed. As in other serves, however, the serve should not be hit close to the midline of the back court. The ball can hit the side wall just past the short line (short corner drive serve), go straight into the back corner of the court, or hit the side wall several feet from the back wall and rebound "around the back corner." Any of these serves will be effective as long as you vary the

Drive serve.

angle of rebound off the front wall from serve to serve and keep the ball low. To do this, the angle of the racquet face at ball contact must change with each hit. To prevent your opponent from anticipating the position of your serve, learn to hit a drive serve to the forehand and backhand sides of the court with equal skill. However, the backhand side is most effective in preventing offensive returns.

If your opponent "moves up" on your drive serve to take the ball before it touches the ground, hit the ball with more angle to the side wall. This will direct the ball farther back into the court and avoid your opponent's reach.

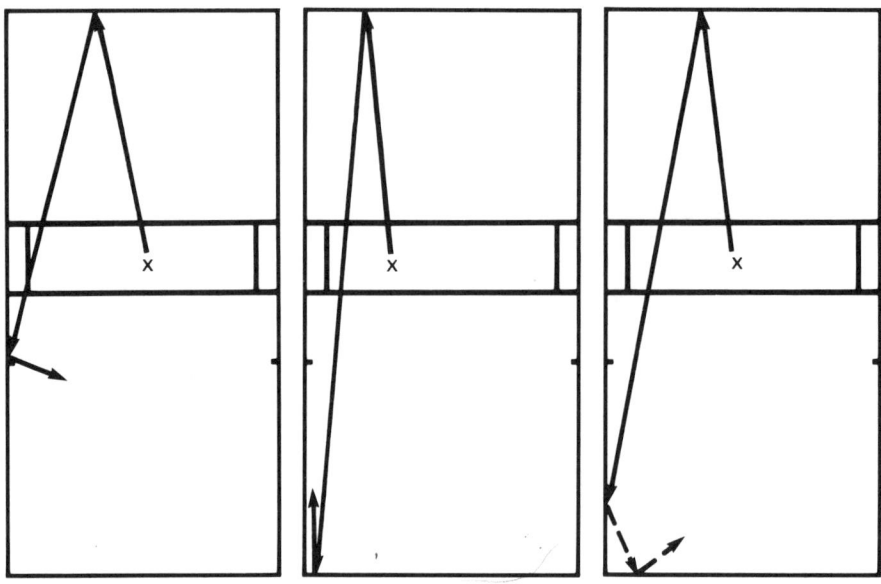

Variations of drive serves: behind short line, to back corner and off side wall.

Z Serve

The Z serve can be divided into two distinct serves — a high Z serve and a low Z serve. The high Z serve is similar to the defensive Z shot in its movement around the court. This serve hits high on the front wall close to the front wall-side wall crotch. The ball rebounds to the nearest side wall, then travels high across the

High Z serve.

diagonal of the court to the opposite back corner. For the serve to be legal, however, the ball must hit the floor before touching another wall (unlike the defensive Z shot) and rebounding again. Thus, the movement of the ball on the court resembles the letter "Z".

This Z serve is hit with the same technique as the defensive Z shot (see page 57). The hips are turned to the side wall, and the forward swing follows a pendulum motion. The racquet face is open, and contact with the ball is made in front of the forward foot. However, the stroke cannot be as strong as the defensive shot because the ball must touch the floor before the opposite side wall is struck. Thus, like the lob serve, the high Z serve needs proper placement and finesse, rather than power, to be effective.

On the opposite extreme, the low Z ball requires power to make the shot work. The low Z serve follows the same "Z" path around the court, but instead of travelling above shoulder height, the ball moves through the court close to the ground. Thus, this serve is hit low to the front wall, similar to the drive serve but with more strength because of the distance across the court that the ball must travel before touching the floor.

The technique used to hit a low Z serve is similar to that for a kill shot (see page 33). The ball must be contacted in front of the forward foot as the weight is shifted forward. The racquet should have a level swing at contact with the ball, and the arm movement must be completed with a follow-through. "Punching" at the ball by stopping the racquet's motion after hitting the ball will only limit the power of the swing. A good wrist snap is also essential in providing the power necessary to hit a low Z ball.

Low Z serve.

The low Z may rebound to the floor anywhere along the side wall past the short line. If the ball is hit hard and close to the front wall-side wall crotch, the ball will rebound to the floor just behind the short line and hit the side wall. The extreme spin on the ball, due to the power of the stroke, will cause the ball to rebound almost straight off the side wall. Thus, an opponent positioned to hit a ball served deep into a back corner will be out of place to return this serve.

If the ball is hit several feet from the front wall-side wall crotch, the ball will be directed toward the back corner of the court. The different angles that can be used to hit the low Z serve depend on the angle of the racquet head when the ball is contacted. The variety of angles provides another means of preventing your opponent from knowing where to set up for the return of serve.

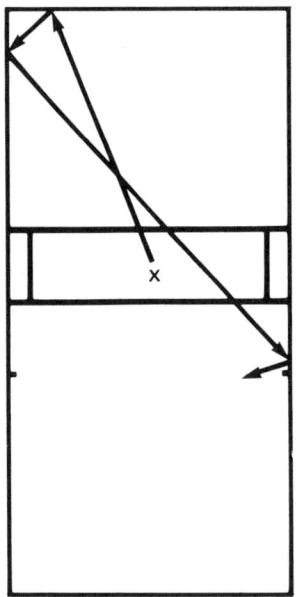
Low Z serve hitting past short line.

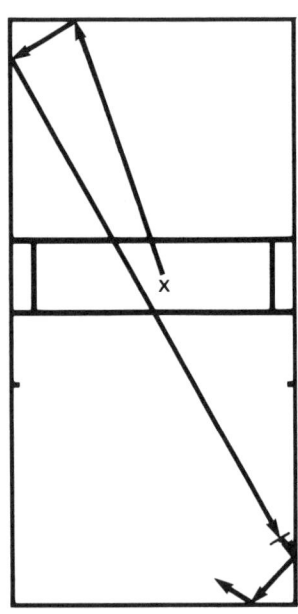
Low Z serve directed to the back corner of the court.

To be most successful, however, the low Z ball requires a powerful and accurate stroke. If the ball is moving too slowly, the opponent may be tempted to hit the ball as it passes through the center-court position. For this reason, the low Z ball is used primarily by experienced players and seldom by beginning players who have not mastered shifting their body weight and snapping the wrist to increase the power of the serve. Beginning players rely on the high Z serve, hit with the pendulum stroke. Although this serve results in a slow-moving ball, it can be especially effective if hit to the backhand of a hard-hitting opponent because it is placed into a back corner.

Overhead Serve

The overhead serve is rarely used in competitive racquetball, but it is a legal serve. It is hit with a stroke similar to that used in an overhead kill, but the ball is not directed as low to the front wall as in the kill shot. The most difficult part of the stroke is starting the ball in play, since the ball must be hit only after rebounding off the floor. Therefore, to be contacted at a point over your head, the ball must hit the floor of the service area with enough force so that it rebounds above your head and outstretched arm. Thus, the ball must be "thrown" to the floor rather than dropped. Because this throw must be done with your non-racquet, i.e., non-dominant hand, the throw is a difficult one to make. If the ball is not thrown straight down, it will rebound out of the service area rather than overhead and cannot be hit. If the ball is not thrown with enough force, it will not bounce high enough for a proper overhead stroke. Therefore, if you anticipate using an overhead serve in a game, the throw should be practiced until its placement is consistent. If the throw is done correctly, the overhead stroke should contact the ball just in front of the forward foot with the racquet held in an extended arm.

To hit the ball with the most control, the server should use a Western grip. The backswing and forward swing of the stroke resembles a circle, much like a tennis serve. The ball should be contacted at a point overhead after you have stepped onto your forward foot and shifted your body weight forward onto the ball of this foot. Until the point of impact, the racquet face should trail the wrist. Upon contact with the ball, the wrist and racquet should be snapped forward to direct the ball toward the bottom third of the front wall. This "snapping" will not only direct the ball downward, but increase the force of the stroke. The overhead serve is completed with a follow-through that brings the racquet downward across the body.

The ball should hit the front wall 3 to 5 feet off the floor. This will insure a low rebound into the back court. If the serve is hit lower, the ball will hit the floor in front of the short line and be

 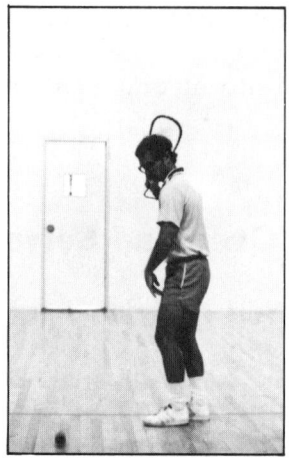 

Overhead serve.

called a fault. This is due to the sharp downward angle of the stroke. To rebound into a back corner, the ball must contact the front wall at least 1 foot on either side of the center when you are serving from the middle of the service zone. The overhead serve offers no unique advantage except a "different" look. Some beginning players like to hit an overhead serve because of its similarity to a tennis serve, with which they are familiar and can hit with power. However, the most difficult serves to return are not necessarily the most powerful, but rather those that are most accurately placed and rebound low into a back-corner position. Because the ball is hit down to the front wall with an overhead serve, the ball will often rebound off the floor with a high bounce. Thus, the ball may not be close to the floor in the back court. Therefore, keeping the ball low to the floor on the serve as done with the drive or low Z is more effective. This is why these serves are preferred by experienced players.

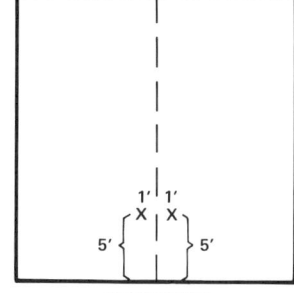

Target area on the front wall for an overhead serve.

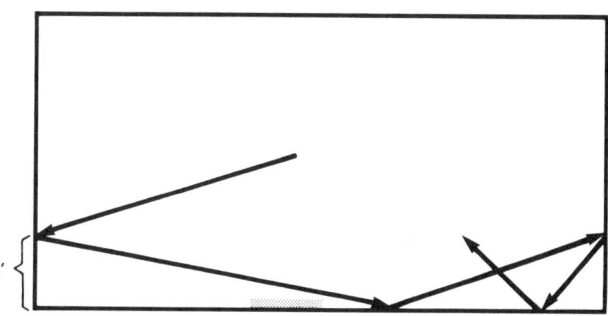

Rebound of an overhead serve off the front wall.

Garbage Serve

A garbage serve is hit with a forehand stroke. This serve "looks" much like a drive serve. The forward swing is level to the floor, and the ball is contacted off the front foot. The force of the hit is dependent upon the speed of the swing and the snap of the wrist when the ball is contacted. The ball should not be hit as hard as it is in a drive serve, nor as softly as in the lob. Yet, the follow-through should draw the racquet across the body to hit "through" the ball. However, the movement of the ball on the court gives the impression that the ball has been mis-hit. Although the ball should rebound wide of the midline of the court, it is not hit low to the floor or high to the ceiling. Rather, the ball rebounds into the back court at a height between waist and shoulder level off the floor. To hit the ball to this height, the serve must contact the ball at a point higher off the floor than for a drive serve or with the racquet face slightly open.

This serve may or may not be hit with enough angle to rebound off a side wall before entering the back court. If it is, the ball should

Garbage serve to back corner.

just brush the back wall so that the ball does not rebound back into play. In this respect, a garbage serve is similar to a half-lob.

If the serve is directed straight into the back corner, the ball must not be hit hard enough to rebound strongly off the back wall. A strong rebound at this point will negate the value of the garbage serve. The strategy behind this serve is to force a ceiling return and/or prevent your opponent from hitting a kill shot or other offensive return. This strategy is especially effective with an opponent who can hit offensive shots consistently off your best serve, placing you immediately on the defensive. Using a garbage serve should at least "get" you past the serve and onto other opportunities to win the point.

Points to Remember:

1. Unless a serve requires a different court position, serve from the center of the service zone with a forehand stroke so that you don't "signal" the type of serve you will hit.
2. Never serve the ball down the midline of the court, where an offensive return is easy to hit.
3. In addition to hitting the serve wide of the middle of the court, hit the ball low unless a garbage serve, lob, or high Z is desired.
4. Serve to your opponent's weak side (usually his/her backhand).
5. Practice serving to the right-hand side of the court in case you play a left-handed player (this will be his/her backhand side) and to provide variation in your serve.

6. Practice hitting your serves to rebound at different angles off the front wall, using varying heights off the floor and changing the power in your stroke.
7. The closer to the center of the front wall the ball is hit, the farther back in the court the ball will strike a side wall. The closer to a front-wall corner the ball strikes, the closer to the front wall the ball will hit the side wall.
8. Use a lob or high Z ball to change the pace of the game and/or force a ceiling ball return.

Common Errors and How to Correct Them

1. My lob serve hits the ceiling or the back wall.
   A. You are hitting the ball too hard or with too much angle toward the ceiling. Hit the ball softer and with less angle, i.e., so that the ball hits lower on the front wall.
2. My drive serve rebounds off the back wall into the center court.
   A. Drop your knees closer to the ground so that you can drop your racquet lower to the floor. This will allow you to contact the ball when it is closer to the floor. Hitting a lower ball into the back court will lessen the chance of a rebound off the back wall. In addition, angling the ball to hit a side wall before it touches the back-court floor should "deaden" the movement of the ball into the back court and prevent a hard rebound from the back wall.
3. My Z ball hits two side walls before it hits the floor.
   A. Hit the ball farther from the front corner and closer to the center of the front wall so that the ball will rebound to a point farther into the back court. Another correction would be to hit the ball with less stroking power while keeping the same scooping forward swing to maintain the height of the ball's contact with the front wall.
4. My drive serve "pops" off the front wall and rebounds high into the back court.
   A. You probably are standing up as you make contact with the ball during the serve. If you do not maintain a low position to the floor throughout the forward swing, the ball will be lifted along with your body and rebound up off the front wall. Make sure that you have followed through your serving motion before you come to a ready position to prepare for the return of serve.

(Continued on page 78)

Common Errors and How to Correct Them (Cont.)

5. My garbage serve hits straight into the back wall.
   A. You are hitting the serve too hard. Take some power off your stroke, and angle the racquet head slightly toward the ceiling upon contact with the ball.
6. My serves go straight down the center of the court.
   A. You are not hitting the ball with enough angle (toward a front-wall corner). This can be corrected in one of two ways: (1) Throw the ball out in front of you and toward your backhand side if you want to hit the ball to the side wall behind you. Throw the ball slightly behind the front foot and toward your forehand side if you want to hit the ball toward the side wall that you are facing. (2) Always throw the ball in the same place relative to your body, but concentrate on breaking your wrist upon contact with the ball if you want to serve to the side wall behind you. Open up your wrist (laid back position) if you want to hit toward the side wall that you are facing. This technique is the best because it will disguise your service direction until contact is made.
7. My overhead serve always hits the floor in front of the short line.
   A. You are hitting the ball too low to the front wall. Check to see if you are hitting the ball just in front of your forward foot and if your racquet head is angled in the direction in which you want the ball to go. If so, then you must aim at a higher point off the floor for the ball to contact the front wall. To do this, don't snap your wrist as much when contacting the ball, and/or hit the ball when it is at a higher point on its rebound.

Chapter Six

Special Strokes and Shots

Offensive and defensive strokes comprise the major part of the game of racquetball skillwise, but there is also a place for special strokes and shots. These skills include: hitting off the back wall, hitting into the back wall, corner shot returns, drop shots, and the volley.

The Back Wall

Up to now, this book has ignored the part of racquetball that makes it an interesting and challenging game — the use of the back wall. Beginning players often "learn to play" racquetball by avoiding the back wall completely. As a result, they are not really playing four-wall racquetball. This type of play puts these players at a disadvantage when facing an opponent who uses the whole court. Without using the back wall as a playable surface, two problems occur: (1) any ball that gets past your position in the court is a lost ball with no chance for you to retrieve it and (2) in order to prevent balls from going behind you, players use many unorthodox strokes with unpredictable results in returning the ball. Thus, when not using the back wall, players must often resort to merely hitting the ball to keep it in play rather than directing it. This is a strategy that we refer to as "Battleball."

When playing "Battleball," the player maintains a center-court position and hits every ball within his/her reach as hard as possible back to the middle of the front wall — the strategy being, if the ball is hit hard to the front wall, it may rebound past the opponent and score a point. Of course, this tactic may work against another "Battleball" player, but the experienced opponent will skillfully use the back wall to keep the ball in play. Only until you feel confident enough to use the back wall will you be able to play more than "Battleball" on the racquetball court.

The key factor in using the back wall well is PATIENCE — having the patience to let a ball intentionally go past you. Before you can play with "patience," you must develop confidence in your ability to play balls on the rebound off the back wall. Part of this confidence comes from many hours of court practice and another part from an understanding of why the back wall is helpful.

The use of the back wall is important because it provides several advantages during the game. First, a ball that goes past you into the back court can still be hit as it rebounds off the back wall. Second, by waiting for balls to rebound off the back wall, you can move into a better position for hitting a forehand or backhand stroke, i.e., setup for the return. If the ball is hit before the back-wall rebound, often it is above or below the ideal hitting area. It is impossible to practice hitting balls at all positions relative to your body. Thus, always adjusting your court position so that the ball is at the same place relative to your forehand or backhand stroke will insure a consistent hit. This means that you will be in control of the ball's movement around the court and consequently your opponent's court position as well. Finally, waiting for the rebound affords you more time to "see" where your opponent is waiting in the court and to plan the most effective offensive return. Thus, the use of the back wall adds to your ability to control the movement of the ball and your opponent's court position and to potentially gain an offensive advantage.

In order to position yourself to hit a good return off the back wall, you must never lose eye contact with the ball or turn your back to the front wall. The most critical mistake that players make when returning balls off the back wall is turning to face the back

Cross-stepping for back wall return.

Special Strokes and Shots

wall when stroking the ball. As a result, a normal forehand or backhand stroke cannot be used because the ball would be hit into a side wall. Thus, out of desperation, the player facing the back wall resorts to flipping the ball over his/her shoulder, hitting a blind shot toward the front. This shot does not allow you to control and direct the movement of the ball — only to keep it in play. Thus, the only way to successfully use the back wall is to pivot your hips for a forehand or backhand return and adjust your position relative to the ball's rebound by cross-stepping up or back. The critical decision to be made when returning a ball from the back wall is whether to use a forehand or backhand shot. This decision must be made quickly, and the pivot to the appropriate side should follow immediately. It is easy to judge the side from which most balls should

Watching the ball as it rebounds to back wall.

be hit. However, balls that follow the diagonal of the court are more difficult to play. Usually these balls begin in the front court and end in the back court at opposite corners. Therefore, a ball that begins on your left side becomes a hit from the right side, and you must pivot to the opposite corner from where the ball rebounds in the front court. Practicing moving for these balls on the court is the best way to learn how to position yourself.

To hit any ball off the back wall properly, a player can never afford to take his/her eyes off the ball from the rebound off the front wall to the back-wall hit. Follow the ball from your pivot position, moving only your head to keep the ball in sight.

Once the pivot to the appropriate side has been made, proper positioning for the rebound will either allow you to "make or miss" the shot. It is hard to learn how to adjust your position for the ball without going into the court and practicing. But a few general guidelines may be helpful in getting you started.

If the ball has touched the floor before it hits the back wall, you must hit it before it touches the floor again, i.e., directly off the rebound. Because it has touched the floor, the ball's bounce is deadened and will not rebound far off the back wall. Thus, you will need to move close to the back wall to hit the ball. However, if the ball hits the back wall without touching the floor, you should wait

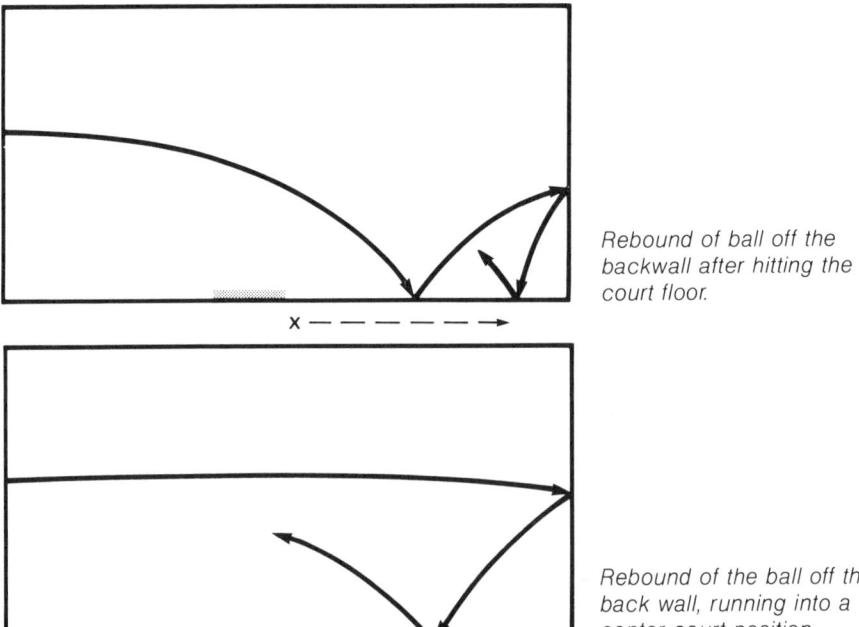

Rebound of ball off the backwall after hitting the court floor.

Rebound of the ball off the back wall, running into a center court position.

for the ball to hit the floor before making contact with it. But be prepared to move forward in the court, because the ball will sharply hit off the wall and "run" toward the front-court area. In either case, you need to position yourself so that at the point of contact, the ball will be hit off the forward foot with the proper forehand or backhand stroking motion.

Backhand return off back wall.

A more difficult shot to return is the back-wall rebound of a lob or ceiling shot that just grazes the back wall and falls to the floor. With either shot, the ball has already touched the floor. Therefore, the ball must be hit immediately after contact with the back wall. The only way to successfully hit this type of rebound is with a sharp wrist snap on the racquet. Station the racquet between the path of the ball and the wall. As the ball passes the face of the racquet, flip

Back wall shot off a ball grazing back wall.

the racquet forward with a sharp wrist motion. Aim the ball to hit a high defensive shot on the front wall so that a weaker shot will still make contact somewhere on this surface. In addition, a defensive return will give you time to reposition yourself on the court.

If during a game these shots are not successfully returned, you may have to hit the ball as it is falling toward you before it strikes the back wall. In this case, the best stroke to use is an overhead ceiling shot (see page 51). With this return, you will keep the ball in play and have an opportunity to later win the rally.

Never jump to hit these balls. All balls will eventually fall to within arm's reach. If the ball hits so high off the back wall that it can't be hit with an outstretched arm, wait for the rebound. Jumping only adds another factor to control when trying to hit the ball perfectly. Jumping for the ball is a sign of IMPATIENCE.

Points to Remember:

1. To hit a ball off the back wall, pivot 90 degrees to the side from which the shot is to be taken, and cross-step forward or backward to a court position where the ball will rebound past you.
2. Watch the ball at all times by turning your head.
3. If the ball touches the floor before the back wall, the rebound will drop close to the back wall.
4. If the ball hits the back wall before touching the floor, the ball will rebound into a mid- to center-court position.

5. Balls that rebound strongly off the back wall can be returned with a defensive or offensive shot using either a backhand or forehand stroke.
6. Hitting a ball that grazes the back wall should be returned by emphasizing the wrist snap and placing the racquet along the wall, hitting a defensive return as the ball falls past the face of the racquet.

Hitting into the Back Wall

A temptation for a beginning player who has learned to rely on the back wall is to hit the ball into this wall rather than hitting it forward off the rebound. This type of hit is more likely to occur if the player turns completely around to face the back wall when playing the rebound. For some players, hitting into the back wall becomes a favorite shot. Unfortunately, the more this shot is relied on, the weaker your game will be. First, it is impossible to hit an offensive shot off an "into-the-back-wall" hit. Second, even defensive shots are unreliable from this return because you are facing away from the front wall, making it almost impossible to "aim" the ball. Finally, with the distance the ball must travel (more than the full length of the court), the ball becomes a slow-moving, easy target for your opponent to return. Thus, hitting the ball into the back wall should only be used as a "last resort shot," when there is no other way of keeping the ball in play.

The only two occasions where this situation is likely to occur (short of your moving lazily to a good court position) is (1) off a passing shot that beats you into the back court and (2) a ball that falls so close to the back wall from a ceiling, lob, or served ball that you cannot place your racquet between it and the wall to stroke it forward.

Hitting into the back wall not only prevents you from taking a better shot to the front wall, but it can be dangerous on the court as well. Standing close to the back wall when hitting the ball may place you in the ball's path, and the rebound off the back wall may inadvertently hit you in the face. Thus, if a back wall hit must be used, contact the ball with an upward scooping motion to angle the rebound above your head. If the ball is hit from a mid- or center-court position to the back wall, your opponent will very likely be in the path of the ball. Standing only 10 to 15 feet away from the ball gives your opponent very little time to duck. Many serious injuries have resulted from this type of play.

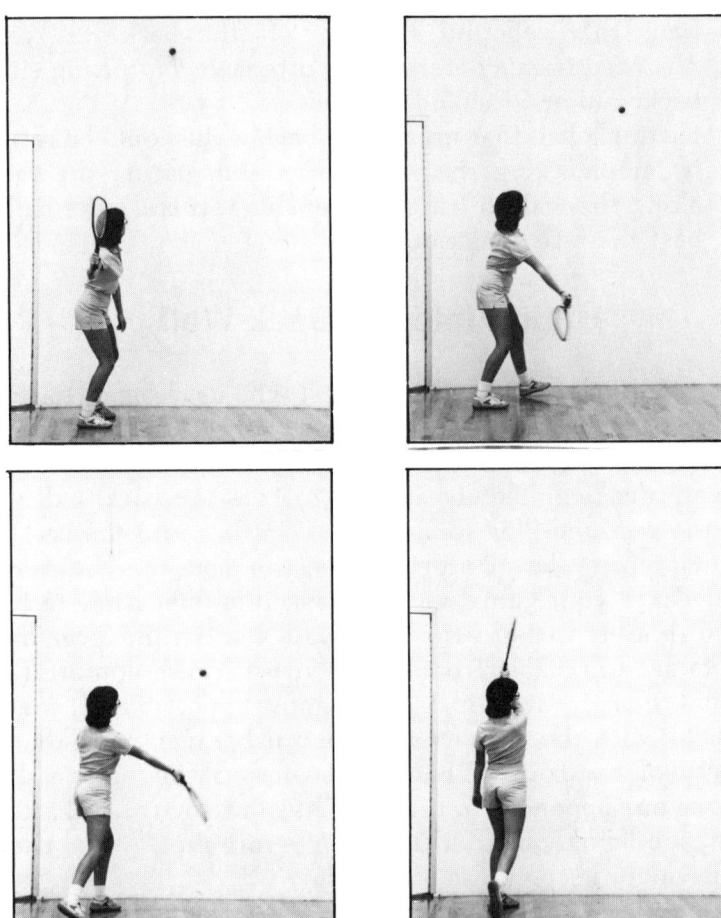

Hitting into the back wall.

The player who wants to win at racquetball cannot afford to rely on such an ineffective and dangerous shot. To avoid placing yourself in the position of hitting the ball into the back wall, remember (1) never turn 180 degrees to face the back wall to return a ball and (2) move quickly to meet the ball in the court rather than being caught out of position with no other shot available.

Points to Remember:

1. Hitting into the back wall is a desperation shot and provides little advantage to the player except to keep the ball in play.
2. Hitting into the back wall should never be done from a center- or mid-court position.
3. When returning the ball to the back wall, use a scooping stroke to lift the ball over your head and past your face.

Hitting into back wall with the player behind you.

Corner Shots

Another important return to learn is hitting a ball that rebounds around a back corner. For most players, this is the most difficult shot in the game. To contact the ball, you must contend with the back and side walls simultaneously. Without any room to stroke the ball, an effective offensive return is eliminated, and you can only hope for a down-the-line ceiling shot.

It is important with a corner shot to pivot immediately toward the corner in which the ball will rebound while keeping the ball in view. The success of this return is dependent upon your ability to position yourself properly in relation to the ball's movement. Anticipate the ball's rebound, and maintain a court position behind the forward bounce. From this position, you can still step into the ball to make contact. If the ball does not rebound with enough force to allow you to hit the ball with a forward swing, then the power in the hit must come from the wrist snap.

The key to a successful corner shot return is having the patience to wait for the ball to rebound off the back wall. Most beginners do not have the patience to wait and swing wildly as the ball comes within reach. Another mistake commonly made is using a wide, sweeping swing with an extended arm, using the shoulder to supply the force behind the stroke. Not only is this "big" arm swing dangerous, but there is no room for this type of "tennis" stroke in the corner of the court.

Contact with a corner hit that has little rebound off the back wall should be made with an open racquet face. This will direct the ball toward the ceiling and force a defensive return. If the ball

Hitting out of the corner.

rebounds away from the back wall, any forehand or backhand return can be used. Most players, however, choose a defensive return because of their back-court position. Therefore, the return of a corner ball should be considered successful if a good defensive shot is hit.

Points to Remember:
1. For all corner shots, position yourself behind the rebound so that you can step into the ball to return it.
2. Avoid using a big arm swing, especially if the ball is rebounding tightly into the corner; instead, rely on a wrist snap.
3. If the ball does not rebound strongly out of the corner, hit a defensive ceiling shot rather than trying for an offensive return.

4. A ball that rebounds hard off the corner may be returned with any type of shot.

Drop Shot

The drop shot is an offensive shot that requires placement, timing, and deception. Therefore, it is not considered a shot for beginning players. The drop shot can be hit with either a forehand or backhand stroke from any part of the court. Most players find it most successfully used from a front-court position when their opponent is in the back court. However, usually the player is not positioned in the front court for the shot but has to move there from a center-court position in anticipation of hitting a drop shot. Therefore, the best ball from which to hit a drop shot is one that rebounds hard off the back wall and runs to the front court.

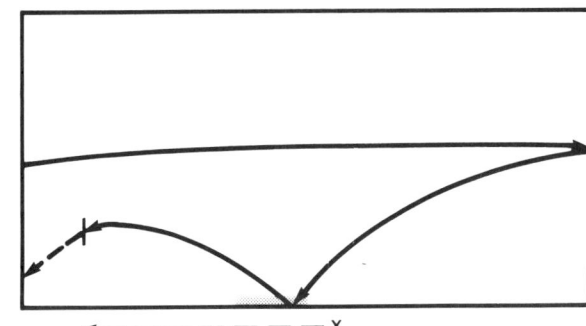

Moving to the front court for a drop shot.

The deception in a drop shot lies in the fact that it "looks" like any other hard-hit stroke. The opponent, therefore, expects the ball to rebound quickly off the front wall. However, at the point of contact, the forward swing is slowed and the face of the racquet is opened. The ball is "touched" with just enough force to return it to the front wall. The "deadened" hit results in a rebound that immediately drops to the floor. If the opponent is in the back court, a well-executed drop shot will not be returned.

To insure the success of the drop shot, try to hit the ball to a front corner. If the rebound is off the front wall as well as a side wall, a ball hit a little hard will slow with the two-wall hit.

Points to Remember:
1. For the most success, a drop shot should be hit from a front-court position.

2. Hit the ball into the corner to insure that the ball will die quickly after the return.
3. Your drop shot should look like a hard return, but upon contact with the ball, the forward swing is slowed and the racquet face is held in an open position.

Open face on the racquet necessary for the drop shot.

Volley

By definition, a volley is the shot that results from hitting the ball after it rebounds from the front wall and before it touches the floor. Any shot can be hit as a volley from either the forehand or backhand side. Ideally, a pivot should be used to insure a proper stroke on the volley return. However, volleys are often mis-hit because the player fails to pivot the hips toward a side wall. This happens because contact with the ball occurs so quickly after the front-wall rebound that there is little time to "setup" properly for the shot. Therefore, hitting a good volley return is not as dependent upon your moving to the ball as it is upon the ball rebounding to the appropriate court position to allow you time to hit it. Thus, every ball is not a good prospect for a volley return. A volley return should never be used unless you are in the proper court position to hit the ball correctly and have a purpose for hitting this type of shot.

Beginning players often use volleys incorrectly to avoid hitting balls that rebound off the back wall. Experienced players, however, use the volley for one of three reasons: (1) to change the pace of the game by speeding up the return to the front wall; (2) to avoid having the ball rebound into a court position (i.e., corner) that would make a strong return impossible; and (3) to force an opponent to hit a return before he/she can regain a good court position. Therefore, the experienced player chooses to hit a volley for a strategic reason rather than because the ball rebounds within reach.

Beginning players hitting a volley with an overhead stroke should direct the ball either to the ceiling for a defensive shot or directly to the front wall in an attempt to pass the opponent. More experienced players may return an overhead kill.

Volleys hit low off the floor provide more opportunity to hit a kill shot return because they are close to the proper hitting position. Thus, even beginning players may attempt this offensive volley with a low rebounding ball, especially if they are holding a center- or mid-court position.

Points to Remember:

1. Volleys should not be hit to avoid using the back wall, but rather to change the pace of the game, catch your opponent out of position, or avoid a more difficult shot.
2. Make sure that you and the ball are positioned for a good forehand, backhand, or overhead stroke before hitting a volley.

Common Errors and How to Correct Them

1. When I try to return a ball from a back corner, my racquet always hits a side wall.
   A. You are using a large arm swing to hit the ball rather than relying on the wrist snap. Place the racquet along the anticipated path of the ball, and contact the ball when it moves past the racquet face using a sharp wrist snap.

2. When I hit a rebound off the back wall, my return always hits a side wall.
   A. Check to see if you are turning your hips to face the back wall rather than only making a pivot toward the side wall. This body position will cause you to hit the ball into a side wall rather than forward.
   B. When hitting the ball, the racquet face may also be directed at a side wall if you are contacting the ball either behind or too far in front of your forward foot. Try repositioning yourself when hitting a back-wall shot so that contact is made with the ball in proper position relative to your body.

3. My drop shots rebound off the front wall and into the court for an easy return by my opponent.
   A. You are hitting your drop shot with too much force. Slow your forward swing more and/or try hitting the ball lower to the front wall and into a corner. With a low corner ball, even a "hard-hit" drop shot should rebound quickly to the floor and out of your opponent's reach.

4. My volleys always hit a side wall before the front wall.
   A. You are either keeping your hips parallel to the front wall when stroking the ball so that your swing carries the ball across your body to a side wall, or you are reacting too slowly to the ball. When reacting too slowly, the ball will be hit behind your forward foot. In this position, the racquet face is open, which directs the ball to a side wall.

Chapter Seven

Putting the Strokes Together: Non-Thinking Strategy

As a beginning player on the court, your strategy is limited by your skill level. As you become more proficient with a variety of shots and feel confident enough to use them in a game situation, your strategy will change accordingly. However, for the most immediate success on the court with beginning skills, a defensive strategy should be followed. This means that your objective during each rally is to keep the ball in play with defensive shots while maintaining a good court position. Points, therefore, are won with this strategy, not because you make an outstanding offensive shot, but because your opponent makes errors in his/her return. At the beginning level, unforced errors account for over half of the points scored. Therefore, if you can keep the ball in play with defensive shots, the odds are on your side that your opponent will lose the rally. This may not be as satisfying as hitting a winning shot, but it is more productive in the end. We call this the "non-thinking" strategy because few decisions are made during play. The only decision that you must make is WHICH defensive shot to hit.

Why are defensive shots a good choice for a beginning player? Simply because these shots are easiest to learn and consistently hit correctly. Defensive shots can be hit hard or soft from anywhere on the court, and there is more room for error in their placement while still being strategically effective. However, to successfully play a defensive game, several points should be remembered.

Concentrate and Watch the Ball

To follow any strategy when playing racquetball, you must concentrate on the game and watch the ball. Any mental distrac-

Concentrate and watch the ball.

tions should be left outside the court to improve your concentration on the game for the players' safety and the fun of the game (see Chapter 10). A player who is distracted by other thoughts may find him/herself at the painful end of a stroke, or at the very least playing below his/her skill level.

Part of concentrating on the game requires that you watch the ball at all times. This is true regardless of whether it is your turn to hit the ball or not. The movement of the ball is so fast around the court and has the potential to quickly change directions that losing eye contact with the ball usually results in an inability to properly "set up" for the stroke in time. Therefore, your return often results in loss of a point because of an unforced error.

To maintain concentration, watch the ball even between rallies when it is in your opponent's hand or during the practice bounces.

Watching the ball.

Putting the Strokes Together: Non-Thinking Strategy 95

Loss of concentration on the return of serve.

Don't let your mind wander so that you "appear" ready to start a new point when you are not. During the rally, anticipate where the ball will rebound, and plan where the most likely return will be hit. Of course, if it is your turn to hit the ball, keep the ball in sight at all times even when you are moving around the court.

Moving and watching the ball.

Serve Your Best

Even though you are following a defensive strategy, you can and should use your serve to its offensive advantage. This means: serve your best. "Best" can be defined in two ways: (1) either the serve that you hit well with predictable results or (2) the serve that may not be skillfully hit but attacks the opponent's weakness in service return. How should you choose between these two options? Usually, the choice is automatic. If a particular type of serve (i.e., lob to the backhand side) always gains a point for you through a faulty return, then use it. If your opponent has no consistent weakness with one type of serve, then use your most skillful serve — one that is always properly placed and hit with authority.

Unfortunately, when playing a new opponent, it will take time and possibly some "lost serves" before you can discover a player's weakness or which serve is working best for you that day. In this case, a good strategy is to serve to the opponent's backhand. For most beginning players, the backhand suffers from a lack of practice because forehand strokes are hit with more success. Therefore, backhand strokes are not as skillfully controlled.

In addition to hitting toward the backhand side, the effectiveness of any serve can be increased if the ball is hit so that the rebound lands close to a side wall in a back corner. This court

Serve to the back corner.

position makes the serve more difficult to return with an offensive stroke. Another benefit of this serve placement is that your opponent must move from the middle of the court to return the ball. Consequently, this court position is open for you to occupy.

If you are still confused as to how to serve the ball, use your own experience as a guide. The serve that is most difficult for you to return will be the most difficult for your opponent as well, assuming that both of you are at similar skill levels. Of course, it does not matter which serve you use if you cannot direct your serve anywhere but down the middle of the court at waist level. Your opponent will always have an easy return to hit.

When practicing, work on all the serves. Some will be immediately more successful than others. Concentrate on these serves during a game. Remember — your service strategy does not suggest that a serve is only successful if it is an "ace." Rather, the serve is useful if a weak return follows (i.e., a ball that is neither an offensive nor a good defensive shot). This type of return sets you up for an easy offensive shot to the front wall and a point.

If your favorite and best serves are not allowing you to even begin a rally, then you will have to change serves. Always keep in mind, though, that your service should never be hit down the middle of the court. If you are still unsuccessful, and your serve is not the offensive weapon that it was designed to be, resort to the garbage serve (see page 75). This serve will hopefully minimize your opponent's opportunity to score with his/her return.

Ultimately, the purpose of the serve is to keep you in a position to score points. One or two serves hit consistently well will do more toward maintaining your service advantage than using many different serves in a game, none of which are hit correctly or placed well.

Keeping a Center Court Position

In a game involving beginning players, balls pass through the center court after rebounding off the front wall. This is because the novice player returns most balls to the center of the front wall. Therefore, if one court position had to be chosen to allow "easy" access to the greatest number of balls, it would be the center court.

Ideally, 1 to 3 feet behind the short line and an equal distance from either wall will give you the best position to reach most balls. A center-court position is suggested not only because more balls travel through this area than any other part of the court, but from here, the player has an equal opportunity to hit balls that rebound short or long or that run along either wall.

How do you gain and maintain this strategic center-court position? If you are serving, the problem is easily solved. When

Center court position.

Service position in service zone.

playing singles, the server usually serves from a position close to the center of the service area. This position is taken for two reasons. First, if all serves are hit from the same place in the service area, there is little chance of the server's court position "giving away" the type of serve that he/she is going to hit. Second, this position allows easy access to the strategic playing position in center court. As soon as the server is allowed to leave the service area, he/she should back up into this area. Because of the server's proximity to center court, a few quick steps will do the job. Unfortunately, beginning players often choose to turn, face the back wall (and the receiver who is hitting the ball), and move to a center-court position while "watching" the serve. Not only is this dangerous because it exposes the server to a direct "in-the-face" return off the receiver's racquet, but a quick return of serve may find the server with his/her back to the front wall as the ball rebounds. Thus, backing up to center court while using peripheral vision to follow the ball is not only the safest, but the most effective tactic.

Trying to "catch" a rebound off the front wall after turning to face the back wall.

Maintaining this court position after the serve is merely a matter of keeping your opponent out of it. To do this, consistently place your shots so that the rebound off the front wall is wide of the middle of the court and deep into a back-court position. A ceiling, lob, or high Z ball are all effective in placing the ball deep into a back-court corner. To return these shots, your opponent must follow the ball to the back court, leaving the center-court position open for you to occupy. As long as your returns are hit in this manner, the center court will always be open.

One precaution that beginners must be aware of is to avoid hitting the ball hard enough to allow it to rebound off the back wall and into the center court. Since the player hitting the ball cannot be impeded by the opponent, a rebound of this type would force you to move out of a center-court position.

Similarly, if you are receiving the serve, hitting a defensive stroke (such as the ceiling, lob, or high Z) along a side wall into a back corner or even a down-the-line return will open the center court as the server chases your return. Therefore, you should be ready to move to the center-court position once your opponent has vacated this area. The usual movement on a racquetball court consists of a constant shifting of position in and out of the center court.

Moving the opponent out of a center court position.

The player who can maintain a center-court position will have the opportunity to dominate the game. This is true for two reasons: (1) offensive shots can be hit from a center-court position with more chance of success than from the back court and (2) the center-court position allows you to take advantage of mis-hits by your opponent that rebound short in the court or hard off the back wall. You may be able to turn these into winning shots.

If you must move from the center-court position to return a ball, then it is important to hit your return away from the center-court area so that you can regain this court position. Beginning players sometimes fail to return to center court after hitting the ball. The faster you can regain this position, the more time you will have to "set up" for the next shot. It may seem to be a waste of energy to move in and out of center court. However, should you choose to stay off-center on one side of the court, you would be leaving the opposite side of the court open for a well-placed shot, and it would be difficult for you to return a ball hit sharply down this side wall. The center-court position keeps either side wall only a step away.

Player out of position for down-the-line hit.

Thus, the non-thinking strategy suggests returning to the center-court position after each shot as quickly as possible, or maintaining this position until moving for a ball forces you out. At the same time, continue to hit defensive shots away from the midline of court to keep your opponent out of this strategic court position.

Moving to the Ball

The reason why you can move your opponent out of center-court position is simply because he/she must leave center court to play the ball. Unfortunately, many beginning players are content to hit the ball if it is within an arm's reach regardless of where the ball is in relation to their body. This means using unorthodox strokes, few of which a player has practiced. Returns hit in this way will serve only to rebound the ball to the front wall rather than place it. This tactic keeps the ball in play but provides neither an offensive nor a defensive advantage. Since you have practiced hitting forehand and backhand shots from waist-level balls, why not use them! The key to success in racquetball is not only knowing where to hit the ball to keep your opponent at a disadvantage, but being able to do it. Using tried and true strokes will produce better game results than a contrived, over-the-shoulder "punch." To hit the ball with

Hitting the ball correctly versus incorrectly.

the same stroke requires that you move to a court position where the best contact with the ball can be made. Usually, this strategy involves playing balls off the back wall to allow the ball to drop from shoulder height as it moves through the court to a lower position off the back wall rebound. Low balls can be hit with the same forehand and backhand strokes by bending your knees and dropping your waist closer to the ground. The stroking technique remains the same.

Instead of waiting for the ball to drop from an overhead position to within arm's reach, however, many beginning players jump to reach the ball. Jumping is never advised as a means of getting to a ball for three reasons. First, all balls will eventually fall to the floor and could be hit from waist level. Second, jumping for the ball prevents you from stepping into the stroke and generating more power in the swing. Third, the jumping is another factor that must be controlled to hit a good return. Therefore, jumping is neither necessary nor practical as a means of moving to the ball. This is one situation where you must wait for the ball to come to you.

Finally, when adjusting your court position to move to the ball for the best hit, it is important to move where the ball will be rather than chasing the ball around the court. Always take the shortest and most direct path to the ball's rebound. If you find this hard to do, spend some time in a court alone, hitting the ball at various angles into the front wall, and watch the ball's movement. For beginning players who have not played a court game before, the rebound angles and movement of the ball must be learned through experience.

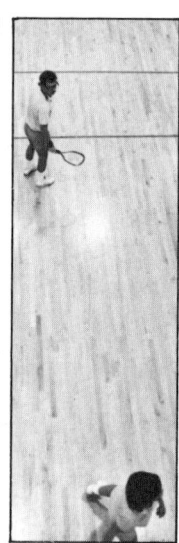

Moving directly to the ball.

Playing the Defensive Game

In summary, playing the defensive game does not mean that the beginning player should never hit an offensive shot. Rather, this strategy tries to simplify the game by minimizing the options available to the player. To some extent, these options are already minimized by the skill of the player and the type of shot available. If an offensive shot can be made successfully, by all means use it to end the rally. However, the beginning player usually must concentrate on merely "staying in the game" and "keeping the ball in play," especially with a more experienced opponent. The defensive game is designed to do this. In general, the defensive game relies only on your ability to hit a defensive shot and keep your opponent away from the offensive center-court position. This means consistently hitting high lobs, high Z balls, or three-wall shots to a back corner while maintaining the center-court position yourself. In this type of game you do not "win" the game so much as the opponent "loses" it. Regardless, you are still the victor. This is "non-thinking" strategy, because your return to the front wall is predetermined before the ball leaves your racquet — a defensive shot to the opponent's backhand corner.

The other part of the "non-thinking" strategy is your court position. Except for the time when you are moving to hit the ball, always station yourself in the offensive center-court position. This means that as soon as the ball leaves your racquet and you can move without interfering with your opponent, return (if necessary) to the center-court position. Too often, a beginning player hits the ball and remains stationary, waiting to see where the opponent will hit the ball. If you are positioned on one side of the court and/or in the fore or back court, you are "giving away" part of the court. A ball hit to the opposite side, short or long, would be almost impossible to return. Therefore, hit the ball and MOVE. Where? To the center court.

This strategy is not only practical for the beginner, but for any player who is facing a stronger, quicker, and perhaps more skilled opponent. The defensive game takes away the opponent's offensive opportunities and slows the tempo of the game. If you are not able to move fast enough to position yourself for good returns, then hitting a defensive return will help to slow the ball's movement and provide more time to get in position for the ball.

Women can find a defensive game especially effective against men. Usually men are stronger and faster and hit the ball with more power. Forcing the man to always return off slower-moving defensive shots will minimize this advantage. In addition, the defensive shot will give you some "breathing room" — time to reposition yourself in the center court and "catch your breath."

Patience — The Key to Winning

The key to playing a successful defensive strategy is PATIENCE: patience to endure long rallies, patience to hit the "sure" defensive shot while waiting for a "sure" offensive shot, patience to move with the ball until it comes to the perfect court position for your best stroke, and finally, patience to let the opponent "lose" the point. The offensive shots are few and far between, and although the defensive game may not appear exciting, it is strategically sound. The player who does not have the patience to follow the game plan who has an itchy "trigger finger," and who tries low-percentage (because of his/her skill level) but spectacular offensive shots will never find this strategy successful. Until you have the PATIENCE to practice and become highly skilled in offensive shots, use what you do the best — a defensive strategy.

Points to Remember:

1. The defensive game is not designed for you to win points, but rather to prevent you from losing points.
2. Begin on the offensive with your best serve or at least with a serve that will prevent your opponent from hitting an offensive return.
3. After the serve, move to the center-court position, and return to it after each hit.
4. Hit defensive shots on all your returns and preferably to the opponent's backhand, if that is his/her weak side.
5. Realize that defensive shots can also slow down the game and help to maintain the playing tempo at a speed at which you can successfully compete.
6. Use offensive shots only if they are "sure" winners; otherwise, you are "giving" away a point.
7. Have the patience to stay with your game plan, and use your skills to their best advantage.

Chapter Eight

Putting the Strokes Together: Thinking Strategy

The "non-thinking" strategy of the defensive game becomes ineffective as a player's skills improve. When a player is able to add offensive strokes to his/her game with a predictable outcome, a "thinking strategy" must be used. The strategy in this type of game not only involves keeping the opponent out of an offensive court position, but takes advantage of the opponent's weaknesses in skill or court position through ball placement and shot selection.

During this game, shots are varied but purposeful. This is a THINKING strategy that calls for the player to use a variety of defensive and offensive shots. Thus, points are won rather than lost, and the style of play is more aggressive. How successful a thinking/offensive strategy can be depends upon the skill level of the players.

How to Choose the Right Serve

Minimally, the "right" serve is one in which an offensive shot is not returned. Ideally, the "right" serve results in no return to the front wall or in such a weak return that the server can hit a winning shot immediately. Which serve will be most effective in achieving these goals will vary from opponent to opponent.

It is always a good strategy to begin by hitting your best serve to your opponent's backhand. Even if he/she is anticipating a ball to this side, the skill of your serve should still score a point. Relying continually on this serve, however, will only give your opponent an opportunity to practice returning it until he/she gets it right! Thus, variety in your serves will be the ultimate key to success at this level of play. How can you add variety to the serve? Changing the speed of the serve, the height to the front wall, the rebound angle to the back court, or the depth to which the ball is hit in the court will all

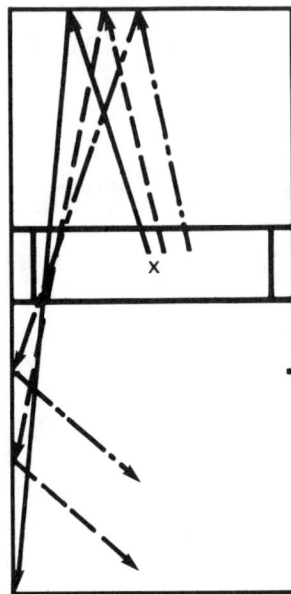

Changing the angle of the serve will cause a change in the depth of the rebound into the back court.

give your serve a "new look." The same basic serve can be hit to either side, short or long, high or low, hard or slow. In general, low, hard-hit serves (like the drive, low Z) are more effective in "forcing" a poor return; however, this type of serve is more difficult to control. High, softer serves such as the lob, high Z, and garbage serve are not as difficult to hit and, due to their placement, result in a ceiling shot return rather than an offensive shot.

Choosing the most effective serve for the game situation varies from service to service and depends on how well you are playing. If the strengths of your game outnumber the strengths of your opponent, you can play your hard serve (drive, low Z) knowing that your skill should win the point. If the opponent's strengths outnumber yours, then you need to play to his/her weaknesses and serve for a defensive return. Continue to keep your opponent on the defensive until an offensive opportunity opens for you. Consequently, the type of serve that you choose will set the tone for your game strategy: attack and try to outgun your opponent or play a more conservative game that keeps the opponent off the offensive.

Don't be afraid to change strategies and therefore the type of serve you hit during the game. You must rely on what is working well for you at the time rather than what theoretically should be successful. But don't give up a well-thought-out plan of attack if your opponent hits a winner off your best serve. The shot may have been luck, or your "best" serve may not have been hit well. Try to vary the height or angle of the same serve. If the serve is hit as you wanted and still a winning return is made, skill rather than luck may be the important factor, and it may be time to find another "right" serve.

You may also serve effectively to your opponent's forehand. Many players practice serving only to the backhand side. Serving

Serving to the forehand side.

only to this side of the court will take away some of the variety in your serve and allow your opponent to anticipate where the ball will be directed.

A serve to the forehand side can be effective if it is properly hit and wide of center. If this is your opponent's strong stroke, then do not serve a hard-hit ball to his/her forehand. Rather, use a lob or high Z serve to force a defensive return. If your opponent does not have a strong forehand shot, a low drive serve will usually force a down-the-line return on the same side of the court. If you anticipate this return and position yourself a step closer to the side wall, your second shot of the rally can be a winner. Therefore, a serve can also be effective if the return of that serve "sets" you up for an offensive shot regardless of how well the return of serve is hit.

Another rule of strategy suggests that when you are tired, hit your hardest serves. Assuming that you are not the player in worse shape, your feeling of fatigue will undoubtedly be matched by your opponent. The harder the serve, the faster it must be reacted to. A tired player reacts slower and/or returns the ball with less power than the fresh opponent. Take advantage of your ability to control

Hitting a kill shot off a down-the-line return.

the tempo of the game by serving hard and keeping up the pressure. This would be an excellent time to hit a short drive serve if your opponent is playing deep in the back court.

Short drive serve.

Remember — with the serve, you control the game. It is the only time during play when you determine where the ball will be when you hit it. Use this advantage to set the tempo of the game, emphasize your strong skills, and force your opponent to rely on his/her weaknesses. At the very least, if a point is not won with the serve, you must be sure that it is not LOST because of a weak serve.

Anticipating Your Opponent's Shot

The beginning player is restricted to playing from a center-court position during a rally due to his/her inability to anticipate ball movement and/or lack of playing skill. Most shots can be easily hit from the center court, and most poorly placed balls generally rebound to this area. Therefore, it is an ideal location for the novice player. The experienced player, however, is usually facing an opponent whose shot selection is varied, and ball control allows more skill in court placement. Thus, rather than "playing the court," as the beginning player does, the more experienced player plays the shot. This means that you should anticipate the best return that your opponent can hit given his/her skill level, and begin moving for the ball's predicted path before it is hit.

Anticipating a shot is not always guesswork. Many players will "signal" the kind of shot that they are going to make merely by their body position relative to the ball. Since you are watching the ball at all times, you can simultaneously watch your opponent set up to hit the ball. Notice changes in stance (hip and foot placement), racquet head angle, and court position (i.e., close to a back wall or in center court). Look for any body or racquet position that is consistent with one particular shot. If nothing is apparent but you are continually beaten by one particular return, use the game situation and court position as a guide as to when that shot would be used, then move to cover it.

Racquetball angle indicating a ceiling or Z-ball return.

There are several situations when any player, regardless of his/her strengths, will hit the same shot simply because court positioning suggests that it is good strategy. These shots can always be anticipated. First is the short return (i.e., drop shot) to the front wall. This shot is used when the opponent is trapped in the back court and the ball is being hit from a front-court position. The player caught in the back court will often rush to the front, hoping to save the return. However, this strategy opens up the possibility of a hard-driving ball or passing shot hit low to the back-court position, which would be impossible to return. To avoid this situation and still salvage the point, the back-court player should rush the front wall (apparently to get to the drop shot), but stop short at a center-court position. With this new court position, the

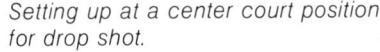
Opportunity for drop shot to the front corner.

Setting up at a center court position for drop shot.

opponent has four possibilities for returning the ball, three of which are good for the receiving player: (1) rush the shot because of the onrushing player, and mis-hit the ball; (2) change tactics and hit the ball hard, hoping to get it into the back court and past the onrushing player; (3) hit a defensive ceiling shot to move the opponent back; and (4) hit a drop shot for a winner. Since the drop shot, if hit correctly, is impossible to return, the receiving player should try to force the first three options in hopes of keeping the ball in play. The worst that could happen would be a point scored off the drop shot, but this would be the likely outcome if the player stayed in the back court or tried to run down the ball in the front court. If the front-court player mis-hits the drop shot, you are close enough to make the return shot. If a passing shot is hit, you can hope for a back-wall rebound. Finally, the ceiling shot provides you with time to move to make a return. At least these options afford you an opportunity to keep the ball in play. Once you have committed yourself to front-court play, almost any ball hit past you would be impossible to return.

The opposite situation can also occur — a ball hit to the back court when a player is "trapped" in a front-court position. Since it is impossible to cover the whole back court, anticipate that the ball will be returned to your weak side (backhand), and move to cover that weak court position. This may also force a hit to your strong side (forehand) in the unoccupied court. If a back wall rebound occurs, you still may be able to position yourself to hit a forehand defensive stroke.

In either case, avoid turning completely around to FACE the back wall when moving to a back-court position. If the ball is returned quickly to the front wall, the rebound may run with you into the back court, resulting in a desperation swing at the ball.

Desperation shot off the front wall rebound.

Therefore, back up away from the front wall, using your peripheral vision to keep track of play.

Finally, if the opponent is out of position to hit an offensive shot (i.e., close to a backhand side wall), anticipate a ceiling shot return to move you into a back-court position. The other advantage to this return is that it provides your opponent with time to regain an offensive court position. However, a ceiling shot also gives YOU time to watch your opponent's movement on the court so that you may potentially take advantage of his/her failure to reposition correctly by hitting to an open court.

To help anticipate the ball's movement, especially how hard the ball is hit, use your ears as well as your eyes. The sound of the ball hitting the racquet can give you a clue as to the power of the stroke. A strong hit will make a louder sound against the strings of the racquet than an easy return or mis-hit. Listen to the sound of the hit to anticipate how hard and fast the ball will rebound off the front wall.

Using the Court Wisely

A player's court position can be used to his/her advantage in two ways. One is to "take away" the opponent's "best shot" — that shot which has a high probability of being a winner — and the second is to keep your opponent moving in the court with the purpose of tiring him/her out.

The first use of the court requires that you maintain a court position to either (1) make your opponent's best return shot impossible to hit or (2) place you in the ideal position to return the ball off this return. This tactic is only important when your opponent has been successful in scoring consistently off one return. To prevent losing more points to this shot, you must in essence "block" it. An example of blocking a shot would be staying to the left of center to "discourage" a down-the-line shot in order to force a weaker cross-court return. To be effective in "blocking" shots,

Blocking a down-the-line return.

however, your court position must be fixed before the opponent returns the ball — otherwise no blocking has occurred. Remember — the purpose of positioning yourself on the court in this manner is to eliminate this shot as one of your opponent's options.

The object of the second use of the court is to literally keep your opponent running. Shot selection is determined not only by the other player's weaknesses, but also with consideration as to how far he/she would have to move to get to the ball. For example, if you have just hit the ball to the backhand side, return the ball to the forehand side. Varying placement of the ball short and long is also effective if your opponent has not anticipated the short ball and set up for this return. Even the most conditioned player will fatigue after long rallies where the ball must be hit from all parts of the court. This tactic can be especially valuable at the end of the game when fatigue causes slower reaction and movement times. Above all, when trying to tire the opponent, keep the pressure on, even during the serve. Don't rush the serve illegally, but quickly return to the service zone after each point without taking an excessive break. Keep the ball moving and your opponent moving after it.

"Returning" to the Offensive Position

Since the serve provides the server with the first opportunity to score, the server is considered to be the offensive player. As such, he/she is initially in control of the game. Thus, it is the job of the receiver to regain the serve and thus the offense. The first step in this strategy requires that you move the opponent out of the center-court position. Any of the defensive strokes or a down-the-line or cross-court return will work equally as well. The preference for the latter two shots is that they are offensive returns and have the potential for ending the rally immediately. However, neither of these strokes should be hit unless the ball is served at knee level or below. Balls that are served high off the front wall or that rebound high into the back court (lob, Z ball, ceiling) should be hit with your best defensive return. With any of these returns, the server will be pulled out of the center-court position, which you can now assume. Consequently, you have eliminated the server's offensive court advantage and regained this position yourself.

Although you should practice returning serves from both sides of the court, most serves will be hit to your backhand. Thus, more time should be spent hitting both offensive and defensive returns

Moving the server out of a center court position.

from this side of the court. To give yourself an advantage in hitting balls with a backhand stroke, you may stand 1 to 2 steps from the middle of the court and turn slightly toward your backhand side. This may "give away" some serves to the forehand side. Therefore, you must always be prepared to move quickly to cover that area.

Waiting for the serve on the backhand side of the court.

Another reason to stand to one side of the center is to have better visual contact with the ball. Since the server will be maintaining a center-court position, standing in the middle of the back court would put you directly behind him/her and block part of your visual field. Standing off-center, you can keep eye contact with the ball throughout the serve and react quickly to the rebound off the front wall.

Finally, to make the best return possible off serves that rebound off the floor high against the back wall, make it a practice to hit the serves as soon after the floor bounce as possible. If you allow the ball to strike the back wall, you must hit the ball as it falls to the floor, possibly very close to the corner. Hitting the serve before it touches the back wall will usually give you a better shot opportunity. Similarly, balls that would "run the corner" should be taken before the corner is hit. Otherwise, you will face a very difficult return. This may mean positioning yourself a step or two closer to the front wall and away from the back wall to catch the bounce.

"Returning" to the offensive can be done in two ways: (1) either hit a winning shot off the return (kill or passing shot) or (2) hit a defensive shot that forces the server to leave the center-court position. The choice of the return will usually depend on the choice of serve. A low ball (below your knee) is a prime candidate for an offensive return; a high ball above your shoulder, a defensive shot. Those balls falling in between should either be taken before dropping below shoulder level or hit after falling below the knee. Balls that rebound off the floor to the back wall should be taken after the floor bounce.

Hitting a Winning Shot

A shot can result in a score for one of three reasons: (1) the ball was hit so well that the opponent could not return it even though he/she was in proper court position (kill shot); (2) the ball was hit to an area of the court that the opponent could not reach in time to return the ball (passing, drop shot); and (3) the opponent just missed the ball — an unforced error. The third reason for a score may be related to your play only if you had consistently hit for long rallies with defensive shots to tire out the opposing player. Otherwise, unforced errors must be considered as being due to a mental lapse on your opponent's part, and you cannot take credit for the point.

However, the first and second reasons for a winning shot depend upon your play. To hit a winning shot, you must be aggressive. Always move quickly to the ball, and align yourself correctly for the proper hit. Never wait for the ball to come to you or be satisfied with hitting the ball if it happens to be within reach if you can maneuver for a better shot.

There are three times when you can consider hitting the ball as it rebounds from the front wall (see page 25). Which you choose depends on how aggressively you are playing and whether you want to speed up or slow down the game. The first is after the ball comes off the front wall and before it hits the floor. Hitting a volley is very effective at speeding up play and possibly catching your opponent out of court position. The best return for a winning shot off a volley is a cross-court or down-the-line passing shot. Care must be taken, however, not to hit the pass so hard that the ball rebounds off the back wall into the center-court playing area.

If you choose to let the ball bounce, it may be hit immediately after touching the floor as it passes between your shoelaces and knee or after the height of the arch is reached and the ball is falling to the floor, passing again through this same area. Aggressive players try to take most balls on the "skip," just after the floor is hit. This also works to speed up play and may catch the opponent out of court position. In addition, it offers the advantage of being at the right position from which to hit an offensive shot.

Waiting until the ball arches and is falling for the second time to the floor not only gives you more time to set up for the shot, but for the opponent to set up for the return as well. Therefore, hitting the ball at this point should be primarily done by the beginning player who reacts slowly to the ball or by the experienced player who is trying to slow down the game.

To hit winning shots not only requires that you move aggressively around the court and return the ball quickly, but that you have a purpose for each hit — a purpose more than just rebounding the ball back to the front wall. Although the ultimate purpose of each shot is to hit a winner, your method of trying to hit a winning shot will differ depending upon your court position and that of your opponent. In general, there are three court positions from which to return a ball: back court, near the short line, and front court.

If you are in the back court, the probability of hitting an offensive shot (kill or pass) is low. Usually your opponent will be in front of you in a more offensive position. Therefore, your best tactic is to hit a ceiling shot to one of the back corners. This will force your opponent back and give you time to move to a center-court position.

If you are at center court, your potential for hitting a winner is increased because of your proximity to the front wall. Even if your opponent is next to you, a passing shot down his/her weak side or to the wall farthest away from the racquet hand is often successful. Certainly a kill to the front wall can score as long as it is hit properly. To increase your chance of success when hitting a kill

Putting the Strokes Together: Thinking Strategy

Passing shot to your opponent's backhand.

shot, hit the ball to the corner farthest away from the opponent and at an angle so that the ball bounces away from his/her court position. If you don't feel confident with either of these offensive shots, you can always rely on a ceiling shot to force the opponent to a back-court position.

Finally, if you are "caught" in a front-court position, several offensive options are available: a drop shot, a corner kill, or a passing shot. Which you use depends on your opponent's court position. If he/she has not "followed" you up to the front court, go for the drop or kill shot. Even if your opponent is able to get to the ball, his/her hit will usually be made on the run and will often be mis-hit. If he/she follows you to the front court, hit a passing shot low to the corner farthest away from his/her court position. If your opponent maintains a center-court position, a ceiling shot may be your only option to prevent the possibility of returning an easy setup should you not have confidence in your offensive abilities.

Regardless of where you are when you hit the ball or what kind of ball you hit, move to cut off your opponent's anticipated return after you hit the ball. There you will be the least vulnerable to your opponent's next shot, and you can begin to set up for another winning return.

Sometimes a Good Defense is the Best Offense

Every player will meet someone who is his/her match against the best serves or who can anticipate the ball's movement in the court and can score at will. Often this occurs when women play men who are more experienced court players and who, due to the speed and power of the strokes, seem to be playing in a different time zone.

The only way to make a game of this situation is to try to outmaneuver the power. This can be done in three ways: (1) slow the ball and tempo of the game by waiting to hit the ball just before the second bounce and by hitting defensive shots; (2) use defensive return shots to the opponent's weak side and hit garbage serves; and (3) keep your opponent out of the center court by hitting balls wide of the midline. Trying to outgun power usually leads to a sloppy game, that which we call "Battleball" (see page 79). However, using a strategy that never gives your opponent anything "good" to hit or a court position from which to hit it eliminates the power as a factor.

Garbage serve to the backhand.

Thus, the best offense for some experienced players against a power player is a good defensive game. It may not have the spark and strong rallies of a power game, but the weaker player who is the tactician will have a chance to score.

This is not to imply that the player can never hit offensive shots, but rather that these shots should only be attempted when there is a high probability of success. Indeed, the defensive game should be used to tire out the opponent by moving him/her around the court, frustrate him/her into an unforced error, or solicit a weak return that sets up your offensive shot. The name of this game is patience — patience to endure the long rallies and wait for your opening to an offensive position. Above all, to use this strategy effectively, you must be careful never to hit a low ball to your opponent's strong side, since that is just the oportunity needed to begin a power game.

Winning When You Are Not the Best Player

Playing the Weakness

Every player has a weakness — a shot that he/she would prefer not to hit. Your job is to find that weakness and take advantage of it if you can. If the opponent does not appear to have a weakness, create one through ball placement and court position. A player who is constantly running to hit a ball will fatigue no matter how good he/she is, so keep the ball moving. If indeed the player is much stronger than you, then go for broke. Try to hit everything and anything, even the best kill shot. If you concede the shot, the point is lost; if you try for the ball, you may just return a few and stop a rally. If nothing else, Mr. Sharpshooter may think twice about his choice of hits, knowing that you came close to returning a ball. This hesitancy may cause some mis-hits and provide better opportunities for making offensive returns. If all else fails and your opponent is hitting winners off your best defensive shots, then your only option is to try to hit with him/her. Continuing to hit defensive shots only postpones the inevitable, so why not try to hit the winner first? If your opponent is not losing points, then you must win them. A few balls may fall and build your confidence and create some question in your opponent's mind as to your capabilities. However, to have any hope that this strategy will succeed, give yourself the best chance for hitting a winner. Never hit the ball and hold court position. MOVE to cut off his/her return, and HUSTLE. Second, don't hit the ball flat-footed. Turn your hips when contacting the ball, and remember to hit through the ball. You will have less chance of hitting a winning shot if your stroke is done incorrectly. Finally, even though you are tired, concentrate on THINKING. Take time before your serve to plan your strategy for the point. Try to finish each point as quickly as you can. The longer your rally, the more possibility of your losing the point. If this strategy doesn't work, at least you put up a fight.

Points to Remember:
1. Play an offensive game, plan your shots, and move your opponent around the court to set up your best return.

2. Vary your serves by changing the force of the hit, the angle off the front wall, and where the balls rebound behind the short line.
3. Anticipate your opponent's shot, and move to a court position to block it and/or set up for the return.
4. Use defensive shots from the back-court position and offensive returns from a center- or front-court position.
5. Keep your opponent away from a center-court position by hitting balls wide of the midline of the court and into the back corners.
6. When you are tired, hit harder and move faster.
7. When playing a stronger opponent, play a defensive game and slow the tempo of play.
8. If your opponent has no weakness that you can exploit, hit with him/her.
9. Throughout the game, take time to THINK.

Chapter Nine

Mental Aspects of Racquetball

The game of racquetball is a fast-moving, exciting drama of action and reaction. The physical efforts required in extending the body to the maximum are certainly important, but the basis for the physical effort is the mind. The mind is an extremely complex part of your total physical self. It controls much of what you are capable of doing in a physical situation.

Combining the mental and physical aspects leads to success in racquetball. A racquetball player must establish a certain mental state if he/she wants to be successful in competing in a game. Your success level must be defined as playing to your absolute maximum level both physically and mentally. You must understand what competition really means and learn how to block out perimeter pressures. You must also learn and develop the concept of skill execution through a "flow" pattern that emphasizes concentration and reduces anxiety and stress. Part of playing within a "flow" pattern is developing an attentional focus and using mental rehearsal and practice. When you use your mental capacities properly in playing racquetball, you will be able to excel physically at your highest potential.

Understanding What Competition Really Means

Competition is a much misunderstood concept related to sport involvement. If a player thinks of winning as the ultimate, the pressure to win in competition becomes a burden that reduces the possibility of winning. However, competition becomes a simplistic concept if a player can envision confrontation with obstacles presented by an opponent. The obstacles come in the form of kill shots, pinch shots, defensive ceiling shots, well-placed Z serves, passing shots, and a combination of shots in a series of strategic placements. The obstacle, or barrier, is the important aspect in competition. The barrier is the shot, strategy, or psychic effort that must be faced enthusiastically; the physical and mental attributes of your opponent are insignificant.

Competition is confronting the barriers and emphasizing internal strife. If you play the game to improve yourself and to execute each shot with as much skill as possible, winning will take care of itself. Worrying about winning is self-defeating; thinking about how others will perceive success or failure is equally damaging. If a shot is executed in a fundamentally sound manner, taking strategy into consideration, then everything possible has been done to win that particular point. The execution of a shot has to be a non-thinking physical effort based on practice and reaction to the barrier presented. If the pressure of winning is permitted to substitute for execution, you will eventually succumb to the pressure. All players lose sooner or later, since there will always be someone better than you on a given day. When the *fear of failure* coincides with the pressure to win, it poses an insurmountable barrier in competition. The pressure of winning and the fear of losing drain your physical energies, contribute to negative thinking, and fail to recognize the important aspect of competing against physical barriers. Concentrating on shot execution as a reaction to a barrier while closing your mind to pleasing someone else will help you to succeed.

Developing the Flow in the Execution

To fully respond and react when playing racquetball requires a *flow*. The games of squash, handball, and tennis all provide a similar feeling of flow that lends an intangible aspect to performance. Flow is difficult to describe, but when you experience it, there is no mistaking that there is an additional ingredient contributing to your play experience. Flow is a feeling of being totally in tune with the environment. Your concentration is specific to the ball, and all surrounding influences are ignored. The opponent is sensed more than visually observed, as clues from his/her placement of a shot or location on the court are absorbed. The opposing player is only a brief encounter that is a larger part of the total movement within the court. As flow occurs, you are not aware of any mechanical skill adjustments in stroke execution. Your mind is so fully directed toward the ball and with reaching it that all shots become an automatic reaction to the barriers placed by your opponent. The intangible feeling of flow helps you to feel that you will execute each shot perfectly. You are in what has often been termed a "groove," where everything attempted skillwise meets with success. Your total attention is caught up in successfully completing each shot. If the skill level of the players is basically equal, the player with the feeling of flow will most likely win due to his/her relaxed and concentrated effort. When a player is in a groove or flow, time, as defined by society, is minimized. What seems to have been only a few minutes of play might actually have been twenty to thirty minutes. A rally that seems to last for only a few seconds might, in fact, have involved one to two minutes. The point is that you are involved with skill execution to the point that all outside thoughts are blocked out and your attention is directed to simply hitting each shot. Flow is not a mystic aspect of playing racquetball, but rather a combination of total relaxation and concentration. If you can learn how to relax and concentrate, not only will your skills improve but you will enjoy the game much more.

Reducing the Feelings of Stress and Anxiety

Anxiety eliminates the possibility of good play in racquetball or any other sport. When you participate in a relaxed, confident state, each shot tends to be acceptable at minimal effort and very good at maximum level. However, when your muscles tense during play, it means that you may be doing any of the following: (1) attempting to perform for an audience; (2) worrying about what someone will think of your performance; (3) overemphasizing winning; and (4) being afraid of losing. All of these are examples of mental thoughts that cause tension. If you begin to think, "I cannot believe that I am doing this well," or "I know I am going to mess up pretty soon," you are proclaiming a self-destructive prophecy. This, in turn, creates pressure to perform, which leads to tension, which ultimately causes your muscles to tense. Symptoms of tension also include sweaty palms, a racing heart, and a restriction of a free-flowing, coordinated bodily effort. As a result, you may miss a hit, which tells you that something went wrong, and you begin to analyze the mistake. Once this happens, your muscles tense even more as the pressure mounts. You respond by becoming even more anxious, and your performance consequently suffers. You experience continual losses, your confidence fades, and you develop a negative attitude.

The cycle described above will continue until you alter it through a concentrated physical and mental effort.

To cope with the stress, you must begin to think in a positive manner and believe that each shot and physical attempt will be successful. With this attitude will come some winning shots followed by even more good play, and with each successful play, your confidence will increase. Renewed confidence is best achieved by playing an opponent who hits paced shots that can be anticipated easily. Regardless of whether you win or lose, if you hit each shot firmly, your confidence will increase, and you will begin to regain form. You must be able to recognize the anxiety cycle; once you can do this, you can perform various exercises that will relieve the tension and permit your muscles to relax. Then you can play in a more fluid manner.

You also should work on developing what are called "coping skills." Eliminating negative thoughts and instead thinking positively serve as a coping tool. If you can emphasize the one good shot and focus on how good it felt to hit that shot, the negative attitudes begin to fade. This reverses the tension and anxiety cycle — performance improves with relaxation, and tension decreases.

The Contribution of Relaxation To Racquetball Performance

The key to muscle relaxation is being able to recognize muscle tension. You experience tension in several muscle groups when engaged in competition. Grasping the racket too tightly will tense the muscles throughout the forearm, wrist, hand, upper arm, and elbow. Tension also occurs in the shoulder area and the neck, and it is commonplace in the jaw and face areas as the pressure increases in a match. Weakness in the knees and legs, shortness of breath not related to oxygen debt, profuse sweating not related to physical exertion, and mental confusion (e.g., not remembering the score after a point) are also signs of tension. All of these symptoms can be recognized and treated immediately during a match. Tension can also be controlled through mental rehearsal, and pre-match relaxation.

Responding to tension during a match requires you to periodically check for tension in muscle groups and for other signs of tension. Tense your forearm and then relax it to determine if your muscles are tense. Similarly, shoulders, neck, jaw, and face need to be tensed and then relaxed. You need to know the difference between being relaxed and tense. Once you have identified the tension, you can begin to eliminate it. A tense forearm, wrist, and hand can be relaxed by easing up on the tightness of the grip, and by removing your hand from the grip and permitting it to assume a limp, bouncy position for a short time. Tense shoulders should be rolled up toward the ears, then rolled up and down. To relieve a tense neck, rotate your head and neck clockwise, then counterclockwise. If you tilt your head back so that your mouth opens in response, or place your tongue on the roof of your mouth and press, the tension in your jaw will be recognizable, and you can relax that area. To eliminate tension in your face, grimace and then relax your facial muscles to create a feeling of relaxation. The key is to recognize the tension, then direct your body to relax. The non-muscle group tension signs are recognizable but can be confused with typical physiological functions. Sweating, weak knees, breathlessness, and loss of memory are symptoms, and you should be aware of them. Take a deep breath and hold it for five seconds before expelling the air. The chest cavity will relax, and the pressure manifested by the symptoms will begin to disappear. Do this exercise several times. Even walking away and taking a brief time-out to regain poise and calm down is advisable. Again, the deep breaths serve a useful purpose not only for your muscles, but also for the various symptoms of tension.

Relaxing the hand while on the court.

Relaxing the shoulders by shrugging while on the court.

Relaxing the neck by rolling the neck while on the court.

Relaxing the mouth area by tilting the head back while on the court.

Relaxing the jaw and mouth area by placing the tongue on the roof of the mouth while on the court.

Relaxing the face with a facial grimace while on the court.

Preparing for the game through *mental rehearsal* also contributes to relaxation by making you confident about your ability to respond to the many different situations that occur in a racquetball match. Mental preparation that builds your confidence reduces anxiety, which, in turn, decreases the muscle tension that interferes with skill performance. One form of mental rehearsal is to correct a skill problem by visualizing a skill error and its cause. You can then "rehearse" the correction over and over as a replay of correct performance. Emphasizing the correction, as an option to the error, reinforces the positive aspect of executing the skill. When that particular situation occurs in a match, you are able to hit or place a shot as you viewed it in the mental rehearsal. Mental rehearsal is also used to plot a match strategically and to review certain shots as you would practice them physically. In all mental practice, you need to retire to an isolated area to assure concentration. You must be very specific and accurate in rehearsing the skill and provide thought implants that are positive and correct.

Responding to tension during a match and rehearsing mentally help you to compete with a minimum of anxiety and consequently a minimum of stress. Another way of reducing anxiety and stress is through *progressive relaxation*. This technique is based on recognizing muscle tension and relaxing groups of muscles. The progression follows a systematic relaxation of muscle groups beginning with the face, and followed by the jaw, the shoulders, the upper arm of the right side, the lower arm, wrist and hand, and a repeat of the left arm. This is followed by relaxation of the upper and lower leg of the right and left sides and an overall breathing sequence. You tense each muscle group, then slowly relax it. Repeat this routine three times in succession, then proceed to tense and relax the next muscle group. Facial exercises include wrinkling your brow, grimacing, pursing your lips, pushing your tongue against the roof of your mouth, and yawning while you drop your head back to open your mouth. Relax your shoulders by shrugging them one at a time to your ear, holding the position, then relaxing. The other areas of the

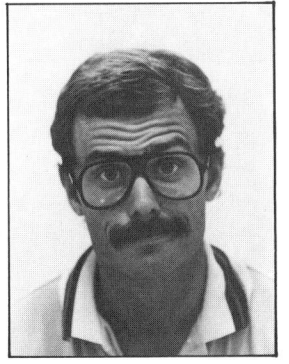

Relaxing the brow by wrinkling the brow.

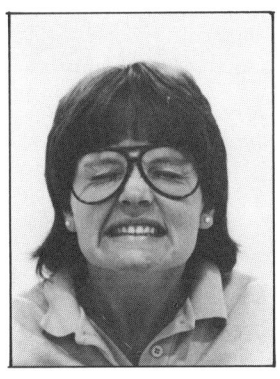

Relaxing the face with a face grimace.

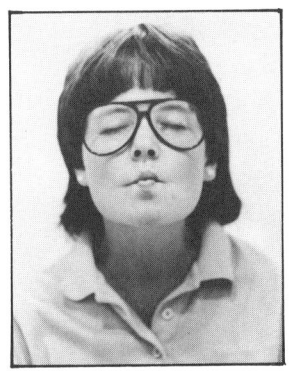

Relaxing the mouth by pursing the mouth.

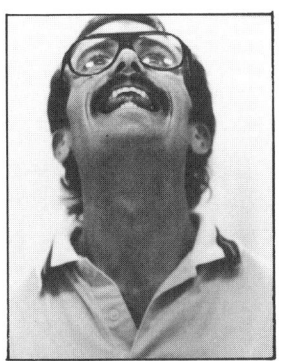

Relaxing the jaw by pushing the tongue against the roof of the mouth.

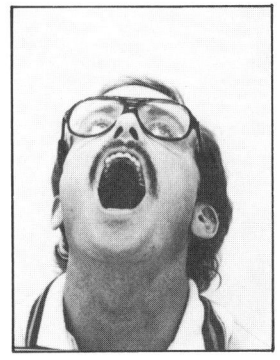

Relaxing the mouth and jaw by yawning and tilting the head back.

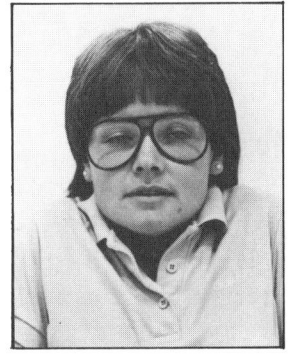

Relaxing the shoulders by shrugging the shoulders.

body are tensed, held for five seconds, then slowly permitted to relax. Work on tensing only the bicep or tricep of your arms and only the hamstring or quadricep of your legs when relaxing those areas.

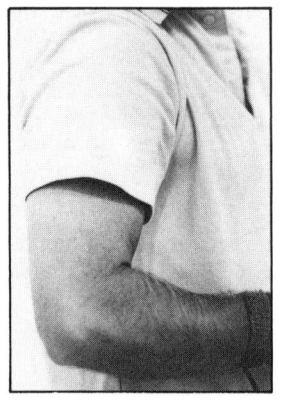

Tensing and relaxing the upper arm.

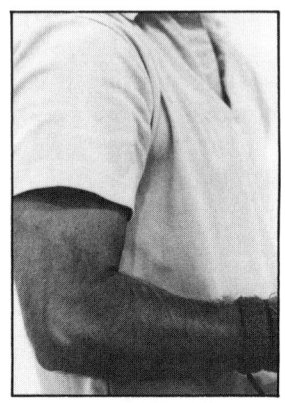

Tensing and relaxing the lower arm and hand.

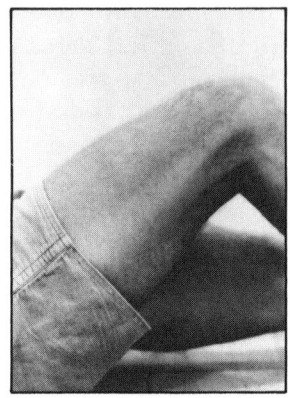

Tensing and relaxing the upper leg.

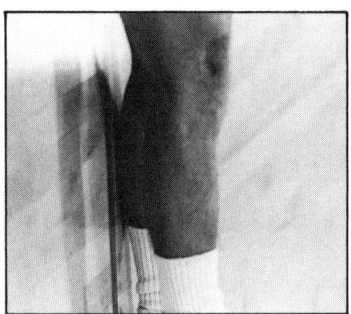

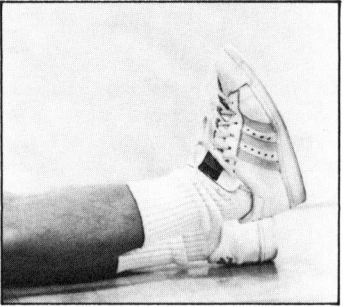

Tensing and relaxing the lower leg and foot.

During these exercises, breathe rhythmically, inhaling and exhaling at a rate of twelve breaths per minute. Close your eyes and let them become heavy. The total time of the progressive relaxation period should be twenty minutes. You need to find a quiet area away from the racquetball courts. After completing progressive relaxation, you may use either mental rehearsal or establish a quiet, relaxed imagery of a favorite enjoyable location (i.e., a blue lake and sky with a gentle breeze, etc.). Mental rehearsal is for the player who needs to develop the confidence associated with practice, while the relaxed imagery helps you to calm down if you are too "keyed up" for a match. The progressive relaxation technique needs to be practiced as a daily habit and prior to a match for the most effective results.

Avoiding Negative Attitudes and Coping with the Opponent's Behavior

Negative attitudes and feelings contribute to unsuccessful performances in all sports, and certainly in racquetball. Responding to a missed shot by becoming upset, verbalizing negative comments, and isolating thoughts on the mistake lead to continued mistakes and cause you to fatigue. The negative comments reinforce the feeling of inadequacy and encourage you to make the same mistake. The waste of energy and production of unnecessary adrenalin will possibly "pump" a player for a short duration, but during the length of a match will drain him/her of needed energy reserves. Once energy is drained, you cannot tap those reserves later in a match or in the second or third match of the day in a tournament situation. In short, the redeeming values of a negative outburst are minimal at best.

The player who uses negative comments that imply weakness also contributes to a less-than-successful venture. Such comments include: "I hope I can break her serve;" "If I am able to win this point, I will win;" "Please don't pass me if I move up;" and "Be careful, don't hit out too much." Each comment contributes to an attitude of compromise, reduction of confidence, and loss of self-esteem.

The opponent's behavior also leads to a response that could be termed "psyching out." Intimidation is used in racquetball by the "back" player striking the "up" player with a shot that will ultimately cause the "up" player to begin flinching on shots from the back court and consequently begin to respond timidly when in that "up" position. The use of gamemanship in questioning calls during a match or taking too much time between points encourages the opposing player to begin thinking negative thoughts. The same psyching effort occurs when time-outs are taken at opportune times and when the opponent takes away the flow of the match. Each effort by an opponent to play a mind game can be offset if a few principles are established. First, you must remember that the real opponent is the barrier that you must overcome to win a point and a match. The opponent's behavior is an obstacle, just as is a skill behavior. Second, you must respond to your opponent by acknowledging his/her effort and concentrating on the task at hand —which is to play the next point. Extraneous aspects of the game like time-outs and intimidating shots are simple diversions that you need to close out of your mind by concentrating on the next shot, seeing the ball, and dealing with the barrier presented. When there is a void in play established by a time-out, or too much time between points, you need to relax by checking the tension of your muscles and then relaxing them. Concentrate on the next series of points and the possible situations strategy-wise that may occur, and focus on the goals of the match. By responding in this manner, your opponent's actions are basically ignored.

Concentration and Attentional Focus

There are four basic attentional focus situations for all individuals participating in a sport activity. The *broad-internal attentional focus* permits you to ponder a particular move and take time in executing a shot or skill movement. The *broad-external attentional focus* allows you to respond to an ever-changing environment by making rapid decisions. A *narrow-external attentional focus* is useful when you must respond to only a few cues. Lastly, the *narrow-internal attentional focus* is for athletes (like runners) who must think introspectively and develop a rhythm for movement as related to the environment.

Of the four types of attentional focus, the racquetball player must not be associated with the broad-internal focus, since he/she must on occasion respond quickly and without thought. The most appropriate and necessary focuses are the broad-external in which the player must develop the skill to make quick or rapid decisions in an ever-changing environment, and the narrow-external focus, when the player must respond to only a few cues. Racquetball is a fast-moving situation game, and the player who can cope using broad-external focus will excel. That player is one who sees the opponent's movement, who sees the type of shot hit with angle and velocity, and who sees the ball in relation to the whole scene. The player with narrow-external focus sees only the ball, focuses on the ball, hears no outside noise, sees nothing that will distract from the shot, and responds to the ball by watching the racquet close on the ball as the ball is hit by the racquet. The individual with narrow-external focus may be able to use that focus to develop a "flow" or rhythm in the match, but seeing the court and the ball and the movement of the game are the most necessary elements of racquetball. Developing broad- and narrow-external skills will enhance your concentration and abilities. Concentration and focusing on the ball as a total effort builds confidence, encourages an elimination of negative feelings, reduces stress, and helps you to develop a relaxed, controlled stroke which, if hit often enough, will win the game.

The mental aspects of racquetball are a major part of the total playing experience, and the player who is most able to use the mind will gain an immediate advantage over his/her opponent. Given an understanding of what competition really is in terms of barriers, the development of the feeling of the "flow" of the game, the ability to reduce stress and anxiety, the ability to relax, the understanding of how self-defeating negative talk is, and the ability to establish the appropriate attentional focus, the beginning and intermediate racquetball player will grow far beyond the levels of the typical peer who simply makes the physical effort only. Racquetball is a game to be enjoyed and savored by using both the body and the mind.

Chapter Ten

Physical Aspects of Racquetball

No racquetball player can use his/her skills and strategy to the best advantage if proper physical conditioning is not maintained. With less-than-optimal fitness, fatigue sets in too quickly, injuries are more likely to occur, and the quality of play declines. The optimal level of fitness for each player, however, is an individual decision based upon the quality of play that he/she wants to maintain. However, conditioning for all levels of play must be a year-round activity.

Physical conditioning is not like riding a bicycle (once you have it, you never lose it). Instead, the state of conditioning is transient and responds only to the amount of use or disuse of the body. If the body is not "used" with exercise, it loses those capabilities such as strength and endurance that exercise promotes. This is not to imply that physical conditioning will help improve your racquetball skills. If you want to be a better racquetball player, you must play racquetball. However, optimal conditioning will allow you to get the BEST out of your skills.

Some aspects of physical conditioning should be trained on a weekly basis regardless of whether you are playing racquetball or not. Thus, when play begins, you are ready to play your best. Most people make the mistake of trying to condition for a sport at the same time they are starting to play. Consequently, this increase in activity overloads the body, and the body "breaks down." Either an actual injury occurs or general fatigue takes away the pleasure of the game. Ideally, the racquetball player should always be "fit" to play.

Other aspects of physical conditioning are important immediately before and/or during the game itself. These help you to keep the activity healthy and safe while getting the most out of your playing ability.

Being Fit to Play: Flexibility For Reach

Flexibility is defined as the ability to move a joint through its full range of motion. Although shots in racquetball ideally should be

Range of motion in the shoulder.

hit just below waist level, there are certainly opportunities for overhead strokes and returns when you must stretch or extend your arm just to reach a ball. Flexibility in the shoulder joint will allow these movements to be made comfortably and easily.

In addition, a player needs freedom of movement through the back to twist and turn, and through the hips and legs to bend and squat. If muscles are tight, movement is limited, and your ability to "reach" the ball in different parts of the court with different strokes is minimized. The use of flexibility exercises can insure that you maintain the maximum range of movement in the joints of your body. These exercises should be done every day. Ideally, if you are going to play racquetball, flexibility exercises should be included as a part of your warm-up before play and cool-down afterward. Flexibility exercises before play help to loosen the joints and muscles to prepare for fast movements of the body during the game. After play, with the cool-down, flexibility helps to stretch

Reaching in racquetball.

muscles that are contracted from exercise and fatigue, thus preventing tight, sore muscles.

The flexibility exercises presented here are by no means an exhaustive list of all exercises that can be done. Your favorites may be missing. Add them in if they are helpful to you. However, the following flexibility exercises are for all the major joints and muscles used when playing racquetball.

Whichever exercises you do, several basic rules should be followed. Start with the head and work down, stretching the large muscles first and then the small muscles. Never bounce into a stretched position. Trying to "force" a stretch contracts the muscle instead of allowing it to elongate. Obviously, this is working in opposition to the purpose of the stretch. To avoid contracting the muscle, hold the stretch position without moving (except to breathe). This static position will bypass the bouncing stretch reflex to contract and allow the muscle to relax and lengthen. Once the muscle is relaxed in a stretch, you may want to try to lengthen the muscle further.

Each static stretch should last 20 to 30 seconds. This means that completing the set of flexibility exercises will take a minimum of 10 to 15 minutes. If you choose to go back and repeat some exercises, plan on spending more time working on flexibility rather than skipping other stretches. If you are excessively sore the next morning after playing, stretch the tight muscles before you get out of bed, and stop and stretch them periodically throughout the day. Many of the following flexibility exercises can be done in street clothes, sitting in a chair or even standing up. You can never stretch too much, and if you are sore, you need to stretch more.

  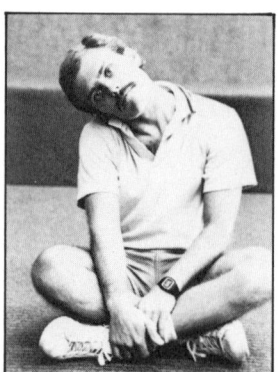

Neck rotation.

Butterfly.

Shoulder stretch (both arms).

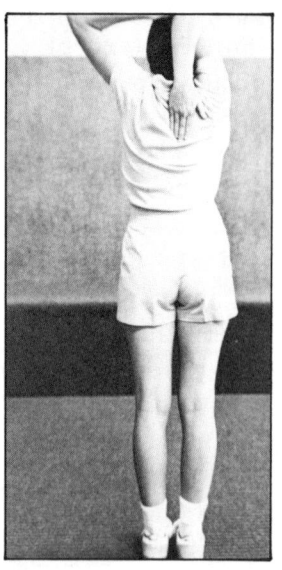 

Back arm lift.

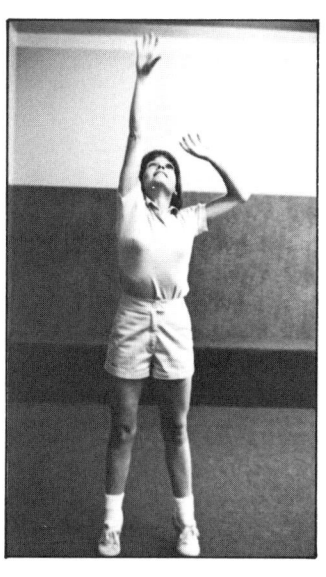

Ladder climb - alternate extended arm.

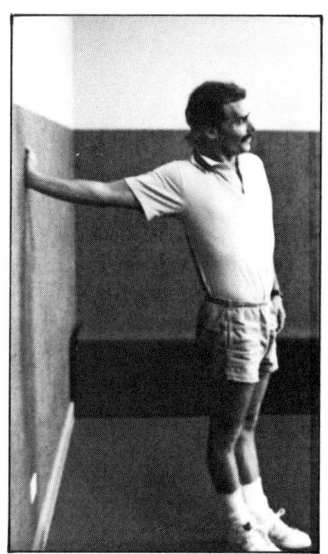

Forearm and shoulder stretch.

Trunk twist (both sides, push against leg).

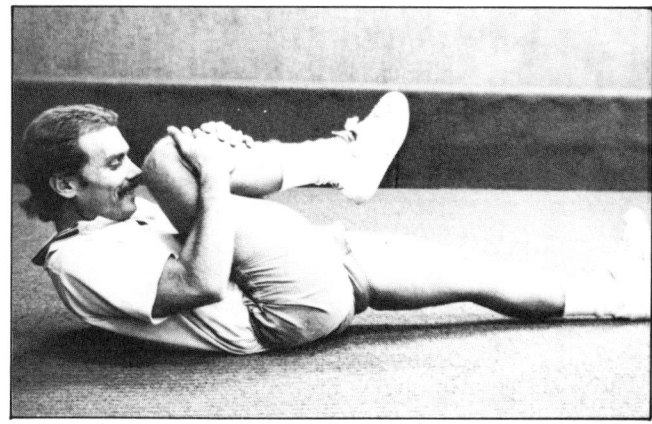

Lower back stretch (both legs)

Hamstring stretch (both legs, keep knee slightly bent).

Ankle rotation (both ankles).

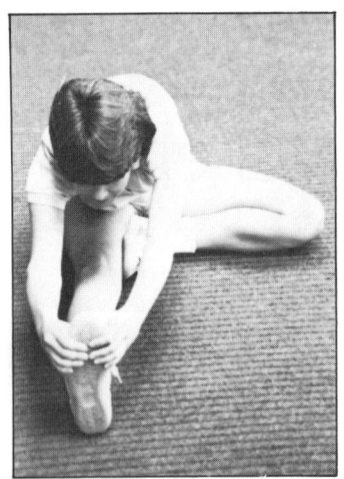

Groin extension (both legs).

Modified hurdler's stretch (both legs).

Achilles and calf stretch (both legs).

Achilles stretch.

Achilles and calf extension (feet flat on the floor).

Wrist and forearm stretch (both hands, most important for racquet hand).

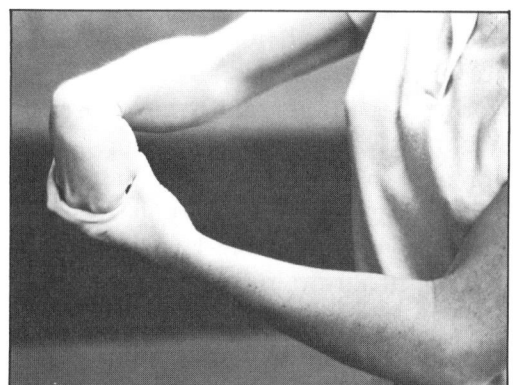

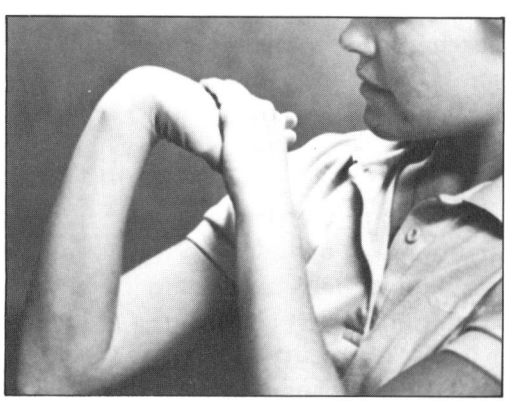

Aerobic Conditioning For Recovery

Although success in racquetball relies on quickness, skill, and strategy, none of these factors will be important if you are too tired to move. During rallies, most of the energy used by the body is a product of anaerobic metabolism — that is, metabolism in our body that liberates energy without the use of oxygen. However, restoring these energy supplies for the next rally requires the use of oxygen. Therefore, although the energy needs during play are not primarily aerobic (requiring oxygen), the more oxygen that can be used between rallies, the faster you can recover and the less tired you will become during the game. This means that part of your physical conditioning program must involve aerobic conditioning — training the body to use large amounts of oxygen efficiently to recover quickly. However, before beginning any aerobic conditioning program, make sure that it is safe for your body.

As a general rule, if you are under 35, have had a thorough physical in the last year, and have no reason to suspect that you are not healthy, you can begin exercising immediately. If you have not had a medical checkup in over a year, suspect that you may be suffering from hypertension or diabetes, are extremely overweight (more than 20 percent over your suggested weight), or have other health problems (back problems), check with your physician before starting an aerobic conditioning program.

If you are over 35, you should have medical clearance from your physician. Make sure that your physician understands the type of program in which you want to get involved. If clearance is obtained, you are ready to begin.

There are five major activities that train your body aerobically: walking, running, cross-country skiing, swimming, and bicycling. These activities are good conditioners, because to perform them successfully requires large amounts of oxygen coming into the body and allows your system to literally "practice" oxygen utilization. Other activities may be suggested as good aerobic conditioners, but they are not as effective in consistently training the body to use large quantities of oxygen. Although any of these activities may be used, a jog-run program is suggested because racquetball is a "running" sport. However, just going out for a leisurely jog may or may not be helpful. Certain guidelines must be followed for aerobic conditioning to occur. These guidelines define how hard you must exercise (intensity), how long (duration), and how often (frequency) for the exercise to be safe, yet hard enough for training to occur.

In general, the intensity of the exercise is monitored by your heart rate. For most people under 35, exercising between 70 and 85 percent of their maximal heart rate will provide an adequate training intensity. Maximal heart rate is the maximal speed that your heart can beat when exercising as hard as you can. One way to predict your maximal heart rate is to take 220 and subtract your age. Once this number is determined, simply calculate 70 and 85 percent of this number. This formula gives you your exercise heart rate range. For example, a man who is 28 years old would have a predicted maximal heart rate of 192 (220 minus 28). His exercise heart rate range would be 134 (70 percent) to 163 (85 percent) beats per minute. Ideally, to train aerobically, you must have your heart beating at a speed that lies within this range.

For individuals between 35 and 50 years of age, the range is slightly different. Exercising between 60 and 70 percent of your maximal heart rate is a good place to begin. Since activity levels in this group are so variable, you can try working at a higher intensity after several exercise sessions if you are in good aerobic condition and if this intensity seems too easy. To make sure that you are not exercising above your capabilities, use the "talking" test as a guide. During the aerobic conditioning, you should be able to "talk" and exercise at the same time. If not, your effort is too hard and you are not bringing in enough oxygen to match the exercise intensity. This means — slow down. If you find 60 to 70 percent too hard, feel free to slow to a lower level. As conditioning progresses, you will be able to move into this exercise heart rate range. But give yourself time to condition for it.

Finally, individuals over 50 should begin at an intensity between 50 and 60 percent of their predicted maximal heart rate. Again, use the talk test previously described as your guide, and regulate your exercise accordingly.

To check your heart rate, exercise for at least 5 minutes, then stop and take a 10-second count of the heartbeats. Use the pulse either in your neck at the carotid artery, directly over your heart, or at your wrist. The first beat that you feel in the 10-second count should be counted as 0. At the end of the time period, multiply the number of beats counted by 6 to see if the equivalent beats per minute falls within the exercise heart rate range. If it is above the range, slow down. If it is below, speed up, unless the talk test suggests otherwise.

Now that you are working at the proper intensity, how long must you exercise at this level? Anywhere between 15 to 60

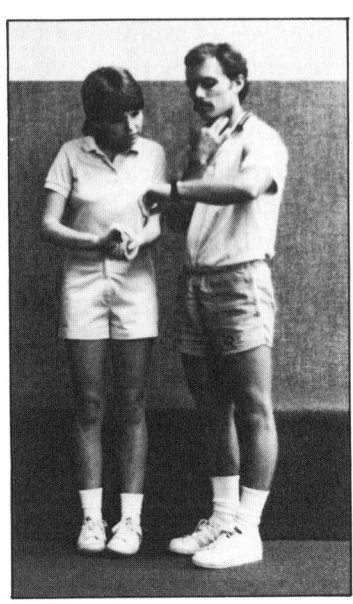

Taking your exercise heart rate.

minutes will provide a length of time to give your body sufficient practice at using oxygen. In general, 20 to 30 minutes is recommended as the proper exercise duration. This means 20 to 30 minutes of constant, nonstop exercise at your exercise heart rate. If you are competing in tournaments and feel that you need more aerobic conditioning, work toward a 60-minute exercise program. However, exercising more than 60 minutes aerobically, except for individuals who have spent years developing their bodies to tolerate lengthy exercise, usually results in an increase in muscle and joint injuries. Since you are using this activity to augment your racquetball play, play more racquetball if you feel you need more exercise.

Finally, how often should aerobic conditioning be done? Three to 4 times a week is ideal — five times is tolerated well. Participating in more than 5 aerobic exercise sessions a week results in an increased rate of injuries to muscles and joints.

To have the exercise sessions be of most value, give yourself between 24 and 48 hours rest between each aerobic workout. The more out of shape you are, the more recovery time needed. However, if your recovery time is longer than 48 hours, some detraining in aerobic conditioning will occur. Therefore, keep your program regular in frequency but sensible in stress in order to balance your exercise needs with your capabilities.

Aerobic conditioning should be a base for all your sports programs and, as such, should be done consistently throughout the year. However, when you are playing more racquetball, you may find that you have to cut back on aerobic conditioning because of time constraints and/or energy limitations. Cutting back to 2 exercise sessions a week will just maintain aerobic condition without developing it. Therefore, if you must decrease your aerobic exercise, maintain at least 2 aerobic sessions a week to avoid completely detraining in this capacity. You won't get any stronger, but at least you should minimize deconditioning.

Many individuals cannot begin an aerobic conditioning program by exercising for 20 minutes without stopping. Bob Glover in his RUN FOR LIFE PROGRAM suggests the following interval method to increase your endurance to the 20 to 30 minutes of consistent exercise. Begin with a 1-minute jog and 2-minute walk alternated for a total of 20 minutes. Do this workout 3 or 4 times a week for 1 week. If this is done successfully, then the next week, decrease the walking interval to 1 minute. Each week thereafter, the length of the jog should be increased by a minute until you can jog for 10 minutes, walk for 1, and finish with a 10-minute jog. The following week, you should be ready to jog for 20 minutes without stopping. Progression from here should never increase the total amount of jogging time per week by more than 10 percent or you will be trying to improve too fast by doing too much.

Never move to the next week's exercise level until you are able to successfully complete 3 to 4 workouts at the walk:jog ratio prescribed. If you find that the first week's exercise is too easy, start with week 2 or 3, depending upon your previous conditioning experience.

Once you are able to complete 20 minutes of jogging, you can add other types of interval workouts to your program. Find a jogging course that climbs hills, or run up stairs to increase leg strength. Change the speed of your run, alternating a fast and slow pace to teach your body to accelerate and recover.

Give yourself 10 to 15 weeks before you begin to "feel" a change in your conditioning. Developing your physical abilities takes time and effort, but you have the rest of your life to work at it.

Weight Resistance Exercise: Developing Strength and Endurance

Muscular strength and endurance help supply the power to your stroke. Without adequate "muscle" behind each stroke, the speed of the ball will be compromised. Muscular endurance helps to maintain this strength during long rallies or through a prolonged match. Therefore, these two muscle qualities go hand in hand and should be developed simultaneously to get the most benefit for play.

One of the best ways to develop strength and endurance is through weight training. For racquetball, this training should be concentrated on the muscles of the arms, shoulder, chest, upper back, and abdominals. How do you know if you have adequate strength in these muscles? First, do you hit the ball consistently as hard as you want, given that your technique is proper? If so, then whatever exercises you are doing are maintaining adequate levels of muscular strength and endurance. If not, weight training may be helpful in developing these muscular capacities.

To judge how much strength and endurance a person should have, Allsen, Harrison, and Vance, in their book *Fitness For Life*, suggest that men should be able to do 17 repetitions using the following weights for the given muscle groups: 1/3 of their body weight with arm exercises (i.e., arm curls), 2/3 of their body weight using chest, upper back, or front thigh muscles (i.e., chest press, lat-pulls, quad lifts), and 1/7 of their body weight using the abdominals (i.e., sit-up exercises).

For women, the same percentage of their body weight should be used, but only 15 repetitions of each exercise need to be performed. If you cannot do these exercises, then two options are available: (1) either gain in strength and endurance or (2) lose weight so that you can lift lighter weights. For the racquetball player, usually #1 is the desired option.

The question, then, is which weight training exercises will be most helpful when playing racquetball? Obviously, exercises that stress the muscles used during play (wrist, arms, chest, upper back, and abdominals) should be included in your program. However, you are only as strong as your weakest muscle, and if your legs are fatiguing despite your aerobic conditioning, you should add exercises for those muscle groups as well. The following is a general list of exercises that are beneficial for strengthening these muscle groups.

Chest Press	Bent-arm Pullover
Upright Row	Wrist Curls
Bent-over Row	Quad Lifts
Triceps Extension	Leg Press
Parallel Bar Dip	Leg Curl

Each exercise should be done with 8 to 10 repetitions for 3 sets. When you can complete a given weight for this number of lifts, you can either increase the weight lifted or increase the number of repetitions per set.

To improve strength and endurance, weight training should be done 2 to 3 times a week (preferably on the days you are not running). Ideally, you should concentrate on improving your strength when you are not playing racquetball often. During your racquetball season, or when court time is more available, strength can be maintained with one hard workout a week. Unlike aerobic conditioning, strength gains remain for a longer time and don't need the consistency of exercise for maintenance.

If you do not have the time or accessibility of a weight-training room, calisthenics can be valuable in increasing muscular strength and endurance. Exercises like push-ups, bent knee sit-ups, and chin-ups done in sets similar to weight training will provide a good stimulus for strengthening. You can begin with 5 sets of 10 repetitions each. Slowly count the number of repetitions done when recovering between sets to mark how long to rest. If this level of exercise is too easy, increase the number of repetitions per set rather than the number of sets until you find a challenging routine.

Stair climbing or bench-stepping can be beneficial in developing leg strength. If you are running up a stairway, give yourself 3 times as long to recover as it took to run the stairs. For example, if the stairs were completed in 10 seconds, wait 30 seconds before repeating the climb. Repeat the stairs as many times as your condition allows.

When stepping on a bench, step up and down with one leg, repeating the movement 10 to 15 times, then switching legs. You may or may not need to rest when switching legs, depending on your condition. Try to complete 5 sets with each leg.

Some improvement in strength may be seen almost immediately (2 to 3 weeks) if you are lifting weights and have never done weight training before. Usually this increase comes from learning to use the weights rather than a change in the muscle. Don't be surprised if after 4 to 6 weeks, the exercises seem harder. They will get "easier" again as you continue to train. If they never feel easier, you are probably overtraining. Eliminate some of the weight-lifting exercises, and continue only with those that you need the most work with. At a later time, the eliminated exercises can always be re-introduced into your training program.

Speeding Up Your Reactions

Many people complain that they don't move well on the court and have trouble reacting quickly to the ball. The best way to improve how quickly you get to the ball is by changing the amount of weight that you have to get "moving." Reaction and movement times can be significantly decreased for the individual who is overweight by merely losing some of his/her body fat. Although dieting can certainly lose pounds, dieting alone usually results in the majority of weight loss coming from lean body mass (muscle). This type of weight loss may actually slow you down as muscle is lost. It is only with the use of exercise that more fat than lean body mass is lost when pounds are shed. Fortunately, the type of exercise best suited to fat loss is aerobic conditioning — the same exercise program described at the beginning of this chapter. However, to use aerobic conditioning to lose weight, exercise for at least 40 minutes, and burn approximately 300 calories per exercise session. Find a good calorie chart for exercise, and estimate how hard you must run, walk, swim, etc. to use 300 calories in 40 minutes. If you can't exercise at that intensity, extend the exercise period so that 300 calories are used but at a comfortable exercise intensity for you. If this intensity also brings your heart rate into the exercise heart rate range, then you will be killing two birds with one stone — losing your fat while training yourself aerobically. If your heart rate is too slow to train aerobically, then opt to lose the weight first. If 40 minutes of constant exercise is too long for you to exercise, begin with Bob Glover's interval program described earlier, and work toward this time goal.

The previous information on the physical aspects of racquetball involved activities and training suggestions to be done throughout the year. This should form a base of conditioning that will give you the strength, endurance, and movement necessary to optimize your skills as a racquetball player. The rest of the chapter provides information on your body's needs both before, during, and after the game that will affect how well these skills are used.

Warming Up and Cooling Down

Warming up involves everything that a player does immediately before a game to prepare to play. Although each player should have his/her own individualized routine to meet particular body needs, some basic similarities should exist in all warm-up routines. All warm-ups involve time for relaxation, flexibility exercises, an exercise to increase heart action, and skills practice. How long each of these warm-up activities lasts varies between individuals and with each individual on different days. Don't be afraid to spend more time on one activity if your usual warm-up time doesn't satisfy your needs.

Relaxation: Most players rush from their job or family commitment to get to the court with just enough time to change clothes and meet their opponent. Consequently, they are tense, and muscles may be tight. It is more difficult to prepare this kind of body for play than one that is relaxed, because the muscle tenseness is working to literally prevent movement. Thus, to get the most out of the warm-up routine, the body needs to be relaxed. This is the time to practice the relaxation techniques presented in Chapter 9. Continue this phase of the warm-up until your heart rate has slowed and you are breathing easily. Once this is accomplished, you are ready to stretch.

Flexibility — the range of movement around a joint — is developed or maintained not only through movement within the sport activity, but as a result of stretching exercises. As mentioned earlier (see page 134), stretching exercises can and should be included as part of your preparation to play. How to stretch was described previously in Chapter 10 (see page 135) along with sample list of beneficial exercises. Merely repeat your sequence of flexibility exercises, emphasizing muscles and joints that have some residual soreness from a previous game or that "feel" tight.

Now that you are relaxed and loose, you need to "warm" up your body to prepare for the hard exercise ahead. Just as you allow your car to idle in the garage on a cold day so that the motor will smoothly accelerate, your "engine" must be allowed to warm up. Shifting the intensity of body movement too rapidly (i.e., from rest to play) may quickly lead to fatigue, as your body cannot adjust fast enough to your exercise needs. An exercise that slowly increases your heart action, such as in aerobic conditioning, will bridge the gap between rest and play. Because space is limited around racquetball courts, running in place, stair climbing, or a repetitive exercise like jumping rope, which uses large arm and leg muscles, can be used to increase your heart action. This heart action exercise should last for at least 5 minutes or until you experience a light sweat.

Finally, you are ready to begin practice in the court with hitting drills. Drills that can be used are listed in Chapter 11. Try to keep

Exercises to increase your heart action.

the ball moving while practicing so that you do not lose the effect of the warm-up. With the same concern in mind, be careful not to finish your warm-up prior to 1 minute before entering the court, or else you will begin cooling down and will lose the beneficial effects of the warm-up. This means be prepared to enter the court immediately after exercising to increase your heart action.

Once play is over, appropriate cool-down activities are necessary to relax the body and prevent excessive soreness in muscles that may not be accustomed to the rigors of the game. The cool-down should begin with the same warm-up stretching exercises that you followed before play and finish with a period of relaxation. Simply follow your warm-up exercises but in the reverse order. Muscles that are fatigued from play and are allowed to "cool off" without stretching are more likely to be sore the next day due to small muscle spasms that result from incomplete relaxation. Your cool-down is not complete if you are still perspiring. Continue to stretch and relax until your body temperature has dropped and sweating has stopped.

Common Injuries and Treatment

Anyone involved in sports at some time will sustain an injury. Racquetball players are no exception. Some of the worst injuries in racquetball occur as a result of collisions between players, a player and a racquet (often his/her own), or a player and the ball. Cuts or lacerations that occur as a result of these accidents usually require minimal first aid. On occasion, stitches may be needed to close the wound. If in doubt, see a physician, especially for cuts in the facial area. In addition, be aware of the symptoms of concussion or broken bones and injuries involving the eyes. These injuries require medical evaluation to determine treatment. In general, use common sense.

More common to the racquetball player, however, are injuries that result from overuse of muscles, tendons, and ligaments. Muscles move the limbs, and tendons hold the muscles in place. Ligaments tie the bones of a joint together. Overuse means that you have pushed your body literally past its "breaking point." This may occur from playing too long when you are out of condition and your muscles are ill-prepared for the effort, or from using inadequate equipment (i.e., worn-out shoes).

The first sign of injury is usually pain, occurring either during play or 8 to 24 hours afterward, followed by swelling around the joint area and tenderness to the touch. This inflammation is usually related to prolonged irritation of the muscle and/or tendon as a result of exercise. Improper warm-up or poor conditioning often contribute to the overuse injury. Sometimes, instead of a chronic wearing down of the musculature, an acute breakdown occurs through improper foot placement or overstretching for a ball. If the injury tears a muscle or tendon, it is called a strain. A tear of the ligament is referred to as a sprain. With either injury, the treatment is similar.

Most sports medicine experts recommend a 5-step program to deal with strains and sprains: rest, ice, compression, elevation, and aspirin. Treatment of the injury should begin as soon as you become aware of your discomfort. Depending upon the severity of the injury, complete rest may not be necessary. Often, players can continue exercising as long as they are careful not to "overdo" and if they ice, compress, and elevate sore muscles after a workout. Worsening pain, inability to move the injured part of your body, or a lack of healing to the injury are signs that you need professional help or need to stop exercising the injured area. A certified athletic trainer can often provide good advice as to the extent of your problem. In most cases, the sooner you treat an injury, the faster it heals, and the more racquetball you can play — comfortably.

Heat and Dehydration

Another concern of racquetball players is overheating. Prolonged hyperthemia (elevated body temperature) may precipitate heat cramps, heat exhaustion, and heat stroke. This problem arises when you are playing on hot courts for an extended period of time and have lost large amounts of body fluids through sweat. Although heat cramps are painful and temporarily disabling, they are not life-threatening. However, heat stroke, if untreated, may be fatal.

To prevent problems associated with "overheating" make sure that you wear comfortable and loose clothing that allows for good air circulation around your body. Rubber suits or heavy sweatsuits merely trap the heat and promote sweating and the loss of more body fluids. Fluids are important in regulating your body temperature by circulating water through the blood vessels, similar to the function of your car radiator system. Decreasing fluid levels in the body in essence drains your "radiator," and you are more likely to overheat. Since sweating is important in keeping the body cool, preventing sweat release is not the answer. Cool air circulating around the body helps. Most important, however, is maintaining adequate body fluids through replacement (i.e., drinking).

A loss of 3 percent of the total body weight may diminish athletic performance. Therefore, if you are playing racquetball for more than 1 hour, you must drink periodically throughout the exercise to maintain your fluid levels. Cold water is best (50 degrees Centigrade) taken in small amounts (3 to 6.5 ounces) and often (at 10- to 15-minute intervals).

Since it is water that is being lost from the body, water is sufficient to replace your body fluids. For most people, electrolyte replacement solutions are not needed during exercise. If proper

Fluid replacement.

fluid levels are maintained as a result of drinking during exercise, overheating will never be a problem. Moreover, you will not fatigue as quickly because of dehydration. A good way to begin each session of racquetball is with a drink of water.

What to Eat and When to Eat

Unfortunately, there is no food that will "make" you an expert racquetball player. However, a lack of food may prevent you from playing as skillfully as you could. The energy needed for racquetball is derived primarily from carbohydrates. Our supply of carbohydrates available for energy liberation is quite limited. Therefore, you need to eat carbohydrates every day to maintain your supply. Trying to play racquetball when restricting your carbohydrates is working at cross purposes. You are asking your body to do something but not giving it the tools with which to do it. If you want to exercise hard, then you must feed your body well. Limiting your intake of carbohydrates will only limit your ease of playing.

In the same manner, playing racquetball at noon when you haven't eaten since supper the night before will cause you to "run out of energy" faster than if you had resupplied your carbohydrates with breakfast. Carbohydrates require only 2 to 4 hours to get out of the stomach and into the bloodstream, where they can be made available to the body. If you know that you are going to exercise, you owe it to yourself to provide the fuel. Eating a meal high in carbohydrates several hours before playing will assure you of high energy reserves. Preferably, these should be complex carbohydrates such as found in fruits and vegetables rather than merely sugar. Make sure to avoid any food that may give you gas or intestinal discomfort.

If you fail to supply your energy needs before the activity, eating during play (honey, jello powder) is useless and may even be detrimental to play. It takes too long to get the foodstuff out of the stomach to help the muscles. In addition, players often find that stomach upsets result from eating. Thus, it is better to eat early and play better.

Chapter Eleven

Drills For The Aspiring Player

Racquetball drills are useful in helping the beginning player develop the skills necessary to play the game and in giving the experienced player opportunity to practice and sharpen his/her shots. Drills may also be used as a part of your warm-up routine to help you get the "feel" for the court and the ball's movement as well as help to adjust your body to exercise.

The following list of drills was designed to provide the player with an opportunity to work on the strokes and shots used most often in a game situation. Evaluative measures are given with some drills to help you determine your proficiency with that skill and when you would be ready to incorporate it into your game plan.

The drills are listed from the most basic skills to playing modified games with an opponent. The beginning player can either start with the first drill and work through to the simulated games or pick the drills that work on the skills with which he/she is having the most difficulty.

In all drills, starting the ball in play is critical. The ball can be either dropped or tossed against a wall. When dropped, you must be sure to drop the ball in front of your forward foot so that you can step into the stroke when contacting the ball. If the ball is tossed to a wall, position yourself so that the rebound falls in front of your body position. This will allow you to step forward to meet the ball. The wrong ball toss will result in learning to stroke at a ball that is improperly positioned in relation to your body.

Scoring scales are presented in selected drills. The illustrations accompanying these drills indicate the size of the target area (1' or 2') and the score allotted to each target zone (5, 3, or 1 points). Balls in the targeted area can be scored by "guess," or small pieces of masking tape can be placed on the floor and walls to outline the areas. Balls that hit a line between 2 point areas should be given the lower of the 2 scores. A legal return not hitting the target area is scored 0 points. Although the target points are somewhat arbitrary, they do identify, through points scored, the accuracy and placement of your shots. In general, the following scoring percentages can be used to determine the effectiveness of your returns and serves:

> 90 to 100 percent of the total points: "bread and butter shot; use this shot whenever your strategy dictates.
> 75 to 89 percent of the total points: consistent enough to use to vary your shots; a dependable shot in a game where you are in control.
> 50 to 74 percent of the total points: be careful — you may miss this shot half of the time; not the shot to choose when the game is close but a good shot to practice when you can afford to lose some points.
> below 50 percent of the total points: POISON — do not hit this in a game situation because you will miss it more than half of the time.

Drill I: Watching the Game

Purpose: To develop a concept of how racquetball is played and the use of offensive and defensive shots during the game.
Method: Go to a court with an observation area, and watch experienced players play racquetball. Count the number of offensive and defensive shots used by each player.

Drill II: Forehand Shots

Purpose: To practice hitting a forehand shot to the back corners of the court from three primary areas of the floor.
Method: Hit 8 balls each from the mid-, center-, and back-court positions. From each position, hit 4 balls to the back right corner and 4 balls to the back left corner. Hit the ball after you have dropped it to the floor.

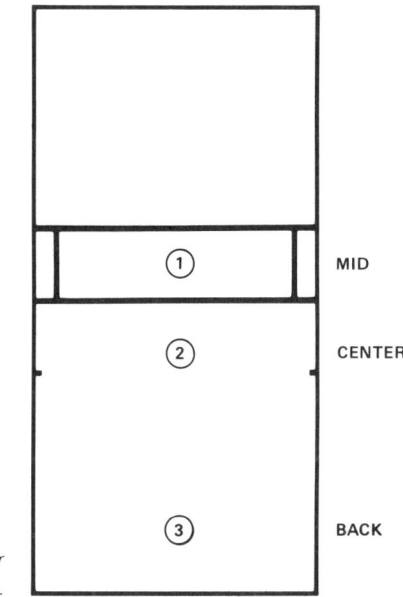

Hitting positions for stroking drill.

Drill III: Backhand Shots

Purpose: To practice hitting a backhand shot to the back corners of the court from 3 primary areas of the floor.

Method: Hit 8 balls each from the mid-, center-, and backcourt positions. From each position, hit 4 balls to the back right corner and 4 balls to the back left corner. Hit the ball after you have dropped it to the floor.

Drill IV: Forehand and Backhand Shots from Side-wall Toss

Purpose: To practice hitting forehand and backhand shots to the back corners of the court from a ball bouncing off the side wall.

Method: Stand with your hips pivoted and facing the side wall appropriate for either a forehand or backhand stroke. Toss the ball into the side-wall. After the rebound, hit the ball to a back corner of the court. Hit 8 balls from each of the 3 court positions, then repeat 8 shots each from the same court positions with the other stroke.

Toss off of the side wall.

Drill V: Suicide Drill

Purpose: To develop muscular endurance and anaerobic capacity, and to practice moving to the ball and returning it to the front wall.

Method: Begin in the center court, and after dropping the ball, hit it to the front wall. Continue to return the ball as quickly as you can, hitting all balls regardless of their court position or the number of times the ball has bounced off the floor. Work at positioning yourself correctly for each hit. Continue this drill for 2-minute intervals, allowing yourself to rest 30 seconds to 1 minute after each hitting session. Continue the drill for 20 minutes.

Drill VI: 30-Second Drill

Purpose: To teach the player to react quickly to the ball's court position and improve his/her movement time, and to work on ball control.

Method: Begin in a center-court position. Drop the ball and return it to the front wall. Continue to return the ball off the rebound, counting the number of times the ball is returned in 30 seconds. Do this drill once every other practice session. Try to improve 1 to 3 shots each time.

Drill VII: Serving Drill — Lob and High Z

Purpose: To practice hitting lob and high Z serves correctly and accurately to a back-corner court position.

Method: Standing close to the center of the service zone, hit 10 lob serves to the right back corner of the court to the designated target area. Score each serve and total the points. Refer to the scoring scale to determine the accuracy of the serve. Total points

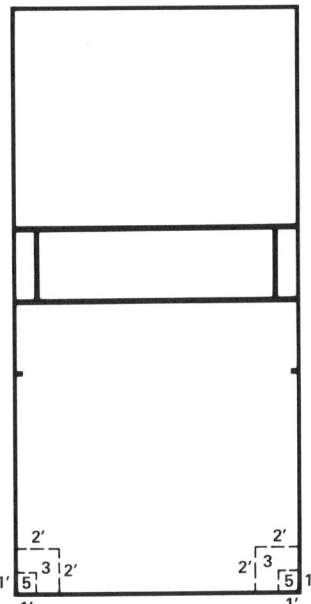

Scoring area for the lob and high Z serving drill.

possible = 50. Repeat this drill with the lob serve to the left back corner and the target area. Score and evaluate. Total points possible = 50. (Note: for a lob hit with a backhand stroke, you may move in the service area toward the backhand side wall). Repeat both parts of this drill using a high Z serve. Total points possible for each part = 50 points.

Drill VIII: Serving Drills — Drive Serve

Purpose: To develop accuracy in your drive serve and be able to drive serve to a variety of court positions.

Method: From the center of the service zone, hit 3 drive serves to each of the 4 designated court positions. Repeat the circuit three

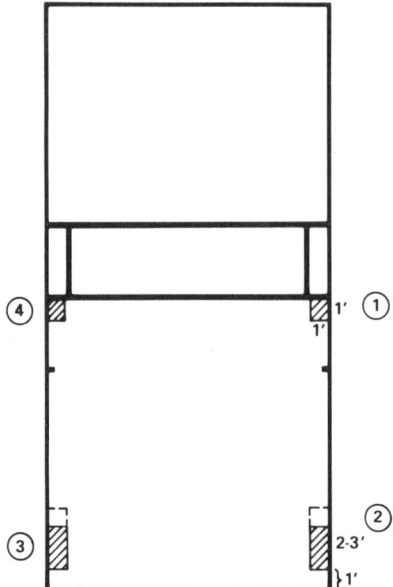

Scoring area for the drive serve.

times. Score 1 point for each correct placement. Total points possible = 36. (Note: you can total points scored to each designated area to indicate your most accurate placement. Total points to each area = 9.)

Drill IX: Defensive Shots — Lob, Ceiling, High Z, Around-the-Wall

Purpose: To practice hitting a defensive shot from 2 court positions and develop accuracy in ball placement.

Method: Using a dropped ball, hit each defensive shot 10 times from center- and back-court positions (5 to each corner). Use the same target area as designated for the lob and high Z serves. Total points possible for each serve from each position = 50. To vary this drill, begin the defensive shot with a side-wall toss.

Drill X: Back Wall Drill

Purpose: To practice hitting balls rebounding off the back wall and accurately return them wide of the midline in a back-court area.

Forehand stroke off back wall toss.

Method: Standing in the back court, toss balls into the back wall to rebound for a forehand stroke. Hit 10 balls, returning each to the front. Score the rebound in the designated target area. Total points possible = 50. Repeat the drill using a ball toss to your backhand side, and return the balls with a backhand stroke. Total points possible = 50.

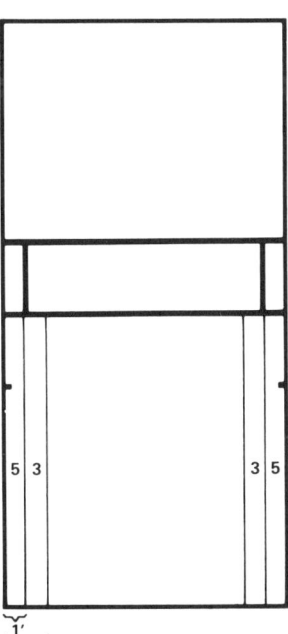

Scoring area for the back wall drill.

Drill XI: Corner Return

Purpose: To practice hitting balls after they have rebounded from a back corner and accurately return them into a back-court position wide of the court midline.

Method: Standing in the back court, toss a ball to your forehand side to rebound either from the back wall to a side wall or in the opposite direction. Return 10 balls with your forehand stroke, then turn and toss 10 balls to the opposite side/back wall for

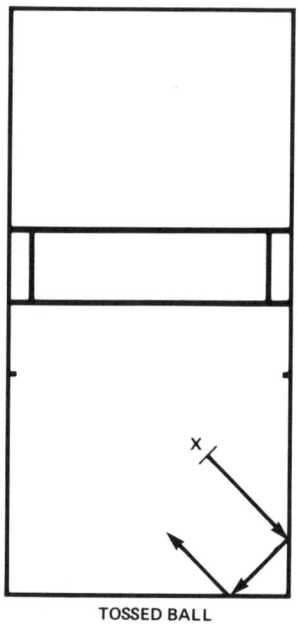

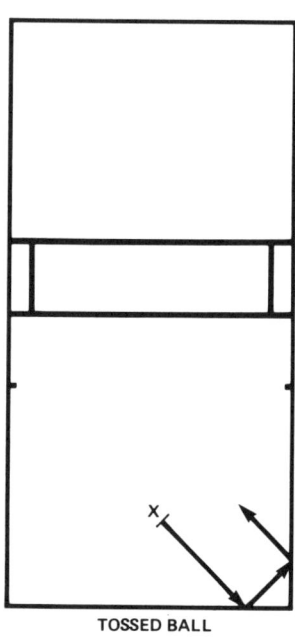

Path of a tossed ball for the corner hit drill - side wall toss.

Path of tossed ball for the corner hit drill - back wall toss.

a backhand return. Hit each ball to rebound into a back-court position and wide of the midline of the court. Score each return with the same designated target area used for the back-wall returns. Total points possible for each stroke = 50.

Drill XII: Repeat Ceiling Shots

Purpose: To practice hitting a ceiling return from any court position.

Method: Standing in a center-court position, use a side-wall toss to put the ball in play and hit 10 consecutive ceiling returns without the ball hitting the floor more than once between shots. Use the designated target area shown in the lob and high Z service drill. Total points possible = 50.

Drill XIII: Offensive Shots — Passing

Purpose: To practice hitting passing shots from 2 court positions and accurately direct them to 1 of two court areas.

Method: Using a side-wall toss to your forehand side, hit 10 passing shots from court positions, A and B. Return the ball into the

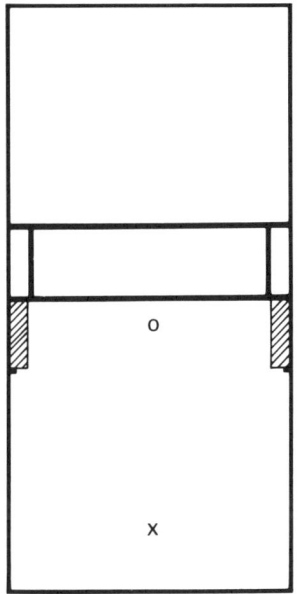

A. Target area for a passing shot for a back court position.

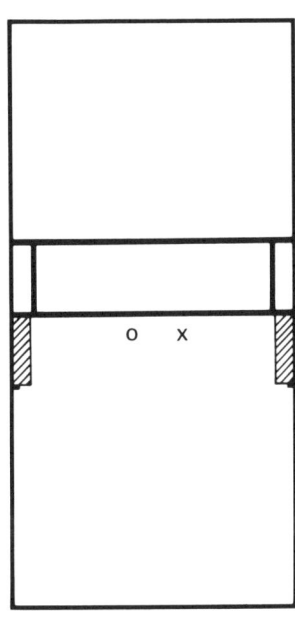

B. Target area for a passing shot from a center court position.

shaded area of the court diagram. Score 1 point for each successful return. Total points possible = 10. Repeat the drill using a backhand stroke. Total points possible = 10.

Drill XIV: Offensive Shots — Kill

Purpose: To practice hitting accurate kill shots from 3 court positions.

Method: Dropping the ball to your forehand side, hit 10 kill shots from each court position: A, B, and C. Score each position

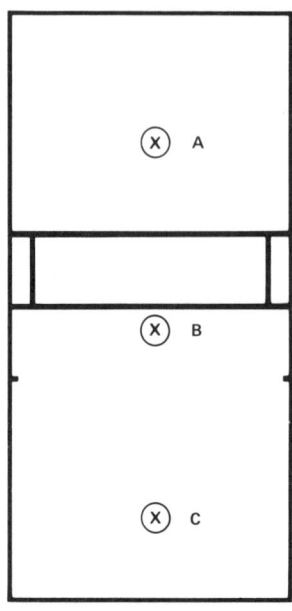
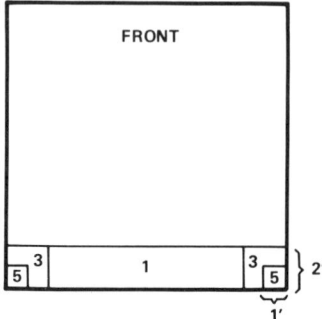

Hitting positions for the kill shot drill.

Scoring area for the kill shot drill.

separately using a front-wall target area. Use corner and pinch kill shots. Total points possible = 50. Repeat the drill using a drop to your backhand side. Total points possible = 50. This drill can also be varied by using a side-wall toss to put the ball into play.

Drill XV: Rally Drill — Hit and Move

Purpose: To practice hitting a ball and moving away from the rebound to avoid colliding with your opponent on the court.

Method: Standing side by side in the back court with your opponent, the player on the right side of the court hits a ball straight into the front wall. After hitting, this player moves to the left and out of the way of the opponent moving toward the ball. The ball is again returned straight into the front wall, and the positions are again reversed. Continue this rotation until the ball is missed.

Drill XVI: Mini Game

Purpose: To give players a chance to practice serving and returning the serve.

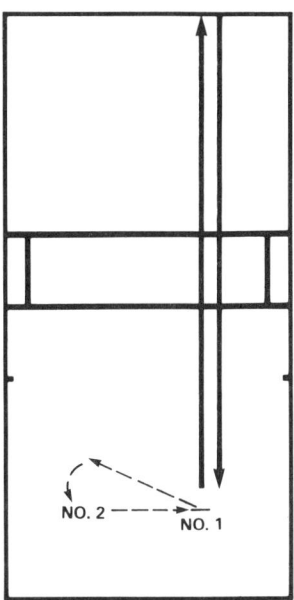

Rally drill to avoid collisions on the court.

Method: Each player serves 5 times and then rotates to the back court to be the receiver. The game is to 15 points, and a point is scored by either player on each rally regardless of whether he/she was serving.

Drill XVII: Defensive Return Game

Purpose: To practice hitting a defensive shot off any serve.
Method: Only the server scores. The server must use a drive serve and the receiver a ceiling or other defensive return. If the receiver does not use this type of return, the server scores a point. If the drive serve is not hit, a side out occurs. Variation: change the type of serve required to be hit, or specify exactly which defensive shot needs to be returned.

Drill XVIII: Game Warm-Up Drill

Purpose: To provide a method for warming up before a game.
Method: Begin by standing side by side with your opponent just behind the short line. Practice hitting forehand strokes to the

Players warming up before a game.

front wall. After several minutes, move two-thirds of the way back to the back wall and practice ceiling shots from this position. Finally, back up to the back wall and hit offensive and defensive returns to the front wall from a ball toss off the back wall.

Chapter Twelve

Court Etiquette and Interpreting the Rules

As in all sport activities, there is a degree of courtesy involved in a competitive racquetball game, and there is a great need to understand and interpret the rules of the game in a fair and objective manner. With two individuals enclosed in a room of 20' x 20' x 40', there is little room for disagreement. The possibility of injury and negative feelings increases if every courtesy is not extended to the opponent and if the rules are not complied with in detail.

Court Etiquette

Court etiquette is imperative to safety, enjoyment of the game, and playing success. The game begins with *etiquette application in the warm-up,* when the court must be shared by players executing the shots to be used in the match. Each player needs to control ball placement to avoid interference with his/her opponent. The court should be divided in length, and all shots should be hit within that boundary. During the warm-up, players should only hit shots that they can control, and they should be considerate of the opponent if he/she must retrieve a ball hit into the front court. Stopping execution of a shot if the opponent walks in front of you or moves to your court to retrieve a ball are specific examples. Bouncing the ball back to the opponent is also appreciated and in good taste.

Once play has begun, *certain situations* require proper etiquette for the players' safety and for enjoyment of the match. Any return of a ball to an opponent should be by bounce only so that he/she can see the ball. When serving a ball, any fault must be called a fault immediately. The call should be projected in a loud voice.

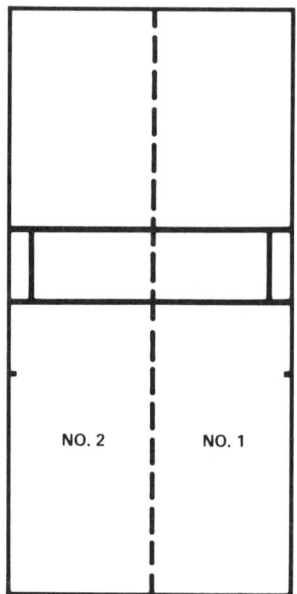

Court divided in length for warm-up.

The most *common faults* are balls that hit the court floor prior to crossing the short line and balls that hit the back wall on the fly. The former call is usually "short" and the latter "long.' The call must be made to protect the "up" player from injury, since once the serve is hit and the "up" player recognizes the serve as a fault, he/she has a tendency to relax and consequently expose him/herself to serious injury. Another reason for making the call immediately is to inform your opponent that the ball is dead. There is one caution in calling faults off the back wall as "long." The receiving player can hit a ball on the fly, thus preventing the ball from reaching the back wall. It

Two players warming up side by side.

Stopping execution of a warm-up shot when a player walks in front of another player.

Bouncing the ball back to an opponent when warming up.

would be extremely bad form to call a "long" prior to the ball striking the back wall, since the call could take away a successful, legal return of serve.

Calling the score prior to every serve is also expected in a racquetball match. The server's score is always called first, alerting your opponent that the score is agreed to by both parties unless he/she stops play to question it. Also, calling the scoring implies that the next serve is going to follow shortly, and the opponent should be ready to receive.

Avoidable and unavoidable hinders are a major part of a racquetball match, and the rules pertaining to the call of hinders are found in the "Official Rules of Racquetball" section and in the interpretation of the rules below.

The *etiquette related to the call of hinders* is, of course, based on those rules. In a friendly racquetball match, an avoidable hinder call should never have to be made. Two individuals playing a match for enjoyment and fitness must be above the subtle attempt to hinder an opponent on purpose. If you play an opponent who intends to hinder, you have the option of not playing that individual again. Unavoidable hinders occur all the time in a game, particularly when a player incorrectly assesses a situation and either moves or doesn't move enough to keep the opponent from gaining a fair chance at the ball. The etiquette of calling an unavoidable hinder rests initially with the player who creates the problem. That player's obligation is to state, "Do you want a hinder?" The response from the other player is either "Yes" or "No." If a hinder is identified by the offending player, the player restricted may say "Hinder please," and the opposing player has only the choice of "Okay." In short, any request for a hinder is to be honored in an immediate affirmative manner. Hinders are to be requested immediately following the infraction so that no question arises concerning whether or not a hinder should be called.

A major safety factor is associated with calling hinders that is crucial to all calls in the game. Any time there is a potential injury possibility, a hinder should be called immediately. There is absolutely no reason for an injury to occur if a hinder is called prior to a player swinging at a ball that endangers the opponent physically. Another

Requesting a hinder.

A hinder when the racquet is too close to an opponent.

part of the etiquette related to hinders is reflected not in the calling of hinders, but in making a concentrated effort to permit the opposing player to strike the ball without having to climb over you. If you can remember that the opposing side must have the opportunity to strike the ball unimpeded, it becomes easier to move out of the way.

Appropriate wearing apparel is not only a part of safety, but also a part of etiquette and rules. The rules require a light color for all clothing, including socks, shirt, and shorts. In friendly games, players sometimes wear dark or blue clothing for something different, but in doing so, you are breaking a rule of etiquette by not giving the opposing side a fair view of the ball.

Getting out of the way so that the opponent has a fair shot.

Contrast of clothing and racquetball ball.

Racquetball has a *"sportsmanship ethic"* that implies that the game is played for exercise and enjoyment. Coupled with that implication is the view that most matches are played without officiating, and it is imperative to call each point or shot fairly and without prejudice. It is doubly important to recognize that no point is worth winning if you or your opponent are injured. The sportsmanship attitude extends to shaking hands following a match and being a "good loser" or "humble winner." The concept of sportsmanship is so much rhetoric in other sports, but in racquetball, sportsmanship is required.

Most racquetball players who advance beyond the early beginnings of skill development will want to measure their skills with others of like ability in some form of competition. Entering a tournament should, and often is, a good experience, but in terms of etiquette, you will be confronted with all sorts of behavior on the part of your opponents. In addition, tournament winners will be required to officiate a match usually following the one participated in earlier.

The *officiating of a racquetball match* requires some degree of understanding of the total game and a specific amount of knowledge concerning the rules. The referee is the sole official in most tournaments, and even in tournaments where linesmen are used, the referee still has the final responsibility for calls. Novice through intermediate play is almost always governed by a referee only. The referee is responsible at the beginning of a match for timing the warm-up, determining which player serves first by a flip of a coin, and making everything ready, including getting a scorebook and towels for cleaning the court, inspecting racquets and playing apparel, and informing players of local ground rules. Referees will sometimes keep score as well as officiate the match. Once the referee completes the specific duties, the match begins with the referee in complete authority. The referee's position, in most situations, is directly behind the court in the observation area. From that position, all calls and appeals are made based on observation. No point may be played until the referee states the score, which is a signal for the server to execute the next serve. Once play begins, players make some calls, with the official serving in an appeal capacity. Players should call their own skip balls and double-bounce pickups. They can request a hinder when an opponent, during a backswing, makes contact with the "back" player, and they may question or appeal a call only in a respectful manner. The referee must respond to appeals for a final decision understanding that there are only three appeal situations:

1. Kill shot appeals when the referee makes a call of "good," "bad," or "skip" and the player affected requests a judgment (see 3.9 a. — AARA Rules).
2. Short serve appeals when the refereee makes a call of "short" or "no call" (see 3.9 b. — AARA Rules).
3. Double-bounce pickups when the referee makes a "two-bounce" call or makes no call (see 3.9 c. — AARA Rules).

The basic key for success when assuming a referee's position is to be consistent, communicate in an audible, direct manner, maintain a decisive attitude, and use good common sense. The referee has sole command over the match in racquetball and possesses one control of the match that is final. It is in the form of a "referee's technical," and it can be executed when a player disagrees or conducts play in a belligerent manner. A technical call results in the loss of a point, and a third technical call can result in a forfeiture. There is little reward in officiating other than you feel that every effort was made to be fair and honest and that the players received a just decision on each point.

Interpreting the Rules

Interpretation of the rules is crucial to acceptable play. The section on Official Rules of Racquetball" provides an in-depth statement of each rule; however, this part of the chapter identifies the most common rules and how to respond to them in a practical playing situation. Some of the rules are quite simple, yet the beginning player sometimes does not initially respond to the obvious and needs to be informed of a rule that most experienced players take for granted.

How to keep score is one of those rules that is taken for granted, yet should be explained. A game is won when the first player reaches 21 points; thus, a score of 21-20 is a legal game. To win a match in most situations requires you to win the best of 3 games. If each player has won 1 game, the third game is played to 11 points, again with the need to win only by 1 point (i.e., 11-10 is a legal score). Some racquetball matches are played to 15 or 11 points in a best-of-five series, and in a class situation, a student may discover that games are played to an assortment of final points to accommodate class procedures.

There are specific *rules governing the service* in racquetball. First, the server must stand between the short line and service line — an area commonly called the service zone. The back foot of the server is permitted to touch but never rest over the short line, and neither foot is allowed to touch or go over the service line. To initiate a

Legal position of the server in relation to the serving zone.

serve, the player must drop the ball and then strike it with the racquet after the ball rebounds off the floor. Following racquet contact on the serve, the ball must strike the front wall first on the fly and then carry beyond the short line. The ball must strike the floor beyond the short line before hitting the back wall, ceiling, or more than one side wall. A serve that strikes the front wall on the fly and doesn't carry beyond the short line, that hits two or more side walls, that hits the back wall on the fly, or that hits the ceiling on the fly is described as a *fault*. Common terms for a fault include a *short* for a serve that doesn't carry past the short line, a *long* for a ball that hits the back wall on the fly, and *two walls* for a serve that hits more than one side wall. A second opportunity is provided for a fault serve. A *side out* serve requires the loss of serve. Loss of serve occurs when the ball does not hit the front wall on the fly after the server hits the ball, or when two faults are served in succession.

Once the *ball is in play*, it must be hit by each player (in singles) alternately. The ultimate goal of either player is to hit the ball so that it strikes the front wall before hitting the floor. A ball can hit the back wall, followed by the ceiling and the side walls, as long as it eventually gets to the front wall before touching the floor.

A server continues the serve for each point played until two faults are hit in succession, a side out serve is made, or the server

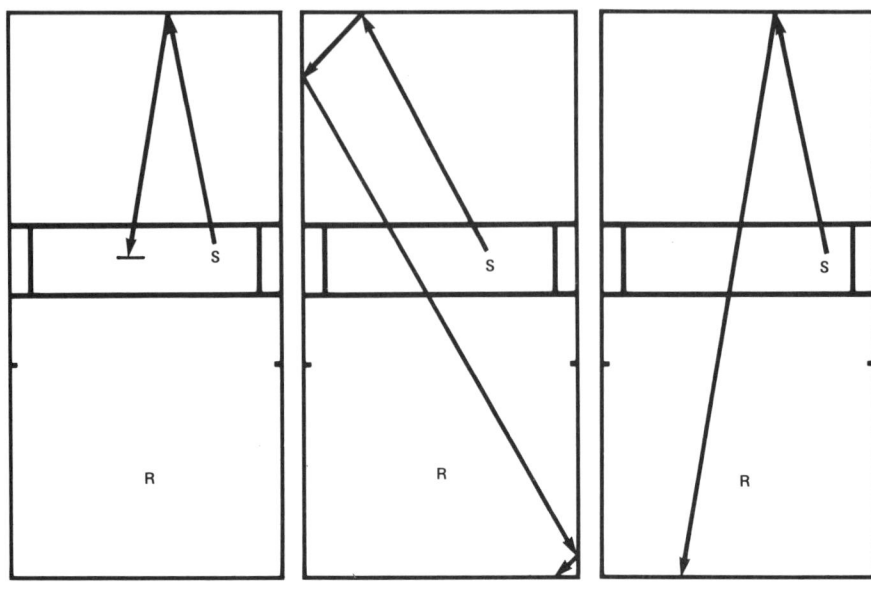

Short serve fault.   *Two wall fault.*   *Long serve fault.*

cannot return the opponent's shot in a legal manner (i.e., not returning the ball to the front wall before it strikes the floor, hitting after the second bounce, or committing an avoidable hinder). A return-of-serve player remains in that situation until the serving opponent has made one of the above-mentioned errors.

Hinders need to be discussed in detail when interpreting the rules. There are two basic types of hinders in racquetball. The *avoidable hinders* are intentional acts of preventing an opponent from a fair try at hitting the ball. *Unavoidable hinders,* commonly called hinders, occur by accident of court play but also prevent the opponent from having a fair chance at the ball.

Avoidable hinders are usually called on a player who intentionally moves in the path of an opponent to prevent him/her from hitting the ball or seeing it clearly. Experienced players are quite skilled at avoidable hinders called *blocking.* The player committing the infraction may hit a shot from an "up" position and then set up to block the movement of the opponent in a "back" position. The movement is subtle and discourages the opponent from making an attempt to reach the ball, since he/she is "back." There are countless avoidable hinders in racquetball. The player who simply will not move to permit an opponent access to the ball is one example. A second example is a player who will move next to an opponent attempting a full-swing shot. That opponent will not be able to

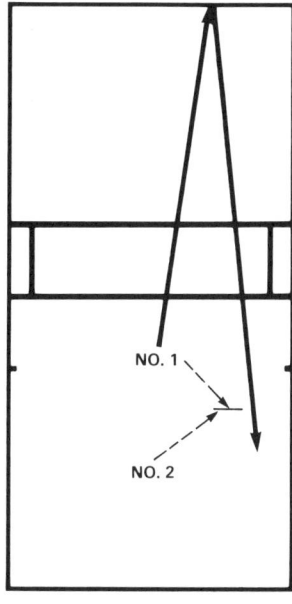

Blocking of an opponent in the back court.

complete the swing because of the position of the other player. A third example is a player pushing or shoving an opponent as a means of giving him/herself impetus to move to reach a ball.

A player moving too close to a player attempting a shot.

A player who doesn't move out of the way.

A player pushing an opponent to get a ball.

Pushing off of an opponent gives him/her an unfair advantage, since it may place him/her in an off-balance position for the next shot. A fourth distinct violation associated with avoidable hinders is the intentional moving of the body into the path of the return shot of an opponent. If an opponent strikes the ball from a "back" position and the "up" player (recognizing that the shot would put that player at a great disadvantage for a return) moves into the path of the ball, the call is an avoidable hinder.

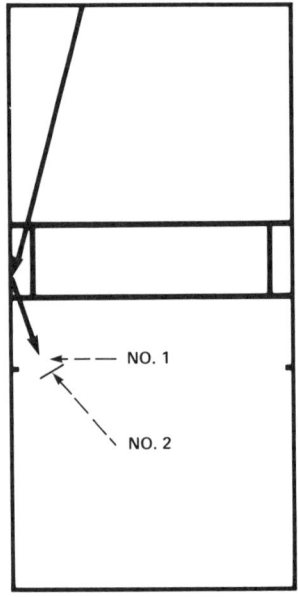

Moving into the path of an opponent, creating a hinder.

Unintentional or unavoidable hinders occur as part of the action of the game and happen without a planned effort. The first example is a *court hinder*. A court hinder occurs when the ball strikes an irregular portion of the court, such as an edge of the door, a can placed in the corner of the court, or any other part of the court that would impede the progress of play. Other examples of unintentional hinders include: (1) a player who is hit by an opponent's shot prior to the ball striking the front wall; (2) a ball that is "shadowed" so that the opponent cannot see the ball clearly; and (3) a ball that goes between the legs of the opponent, thus distracting the player hitting the ball. In addition, when two players collide attempting to move out of the way of each other or the ball, or attempting to reach the ball, play is stopped and a hinder is called.

An avoidable hinder results in a point loss to the opponent if the opponent was receiving and committed the infraction, and a

Court Etiquette and Interpreting the Rules

A court hinder with the ball hitting a ball can.

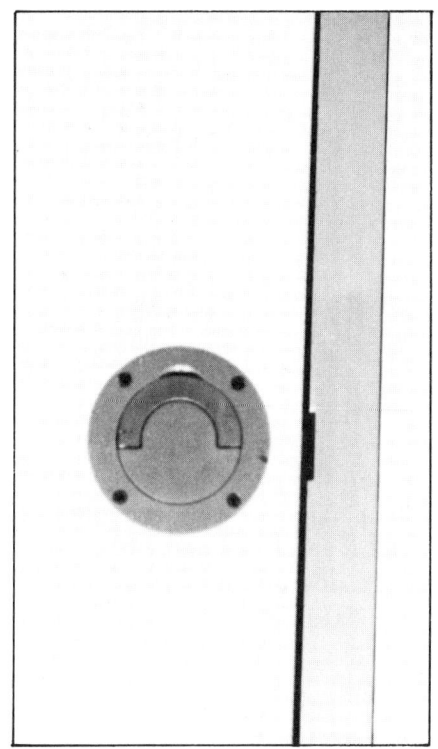

Edge of door court hinder.

Shadowing the ball hinder.

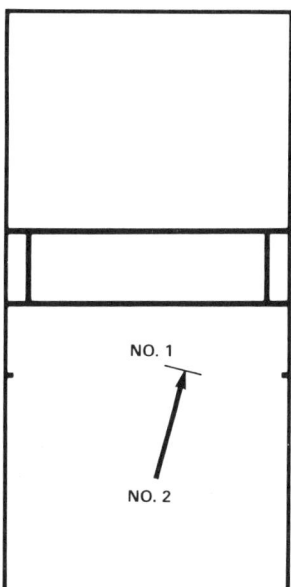

Being hit by an opponent's shot.

A straddle ball hinder. *Two players colliding.*

side out if the infraction was made by the server. An unintentional hinder requires a replay of the point. In a "friendly" game, avoidable hinders should never happen, since the idea of the game is to play for enjoyment and fitness. If a player does resort to avoidable hinders in such an environment, a judicial response is to not play that person again. All unintentional hinders should be called immediately rather than at the end of a rally, and either player may request the hinder.

The necessary rules interpretations include the use of the racquet. Often, beginners are not aware that the racquet must be held in one hand and remain in that hand throughout any specific rally. The racquet must also be attached to the wrist by the thong in order to reduce the possibility of injury. Another interpretation that is common knowledge, but that often is misunderstood, is that the ball must always be struck only by the racquet for a legal return. Other commonly misunderstood rules include the following:

1. The ball must be dry before being placed in play.
2. A server may not take a running stride to execute the serve.
3. A receiver of serve may not cross the imaginary line until the served ball has crossed the short line, thus eliminating a potentially hazardous situation. The *imaginary five-foot line* is a three-inch vertical line placed on each side wall directly behind the short-line position.
4. A *crotch shot* strikes the floor and a wall simultaneously. During a serve, a crotch shot off the front wall is a side out serve. A crotch shot served that strikes off the back wall is in play. During play, a crotch shot is always in play unless it hits the front wall.
5. Only the server is permitted to score after a winning rally.

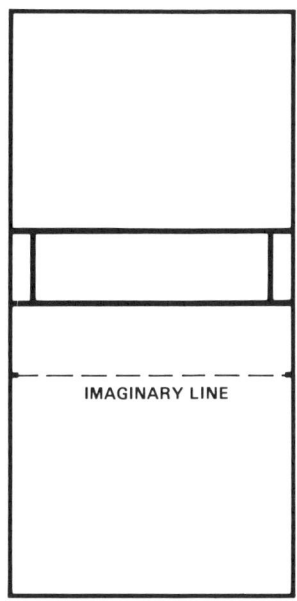

Five foot imaginary line.

IMAGINARY LINE

Vertical line describing the five foot line.

Understanding the common rules of serving, hinders, and scoring allows the novice freedom to play the game early in his/her skill development.

The singles match in racquetball is the only game recommended for safe, enjoyable play, but there are two other games associated with racquetball and rules interpretation. One is called *doubles* and should be played on a regulation doubles court that is larger than a traditional singles court. The other game, played with three players, is called *cut throat.* Rules that relate to doubles are distinct in some ways, including serving order, player hitting order, position during serve, and hinder situations. The serve order follows a sequence of one partner serving consecutive points until a side out occurs, and then the second partner serving in a similar fashion until a second side out takes place. There is one exception to the service order of the partners, and that fits only the first serving team. The first partner serves to the conclusion of serve, then the team exchanges with the receiving team. When the first serving team returns for the second round of serves, the first serving partner again begins serve, followed by the normal sequence of partner serve rotation. The player-hitting order, once the ball is placed in play by a serve, is the same as in the singles game, with team A hitting a serve, team B returning serve, team A responding to return of serve, etc. Either player on a team may hit for that team in the rally.

During a serve, the serving team stands within the service zone as in the singles play experience. One partner serves, and the other partner is directed to stand in the service box. If the partner in the doubles box is struck by his/her partner's serve, the serve is

Doubles serve position.

declared "dead," and the serve is executed again. Once the partner steps out of the box, any ball hit by the serving partner that touches the other partner is a side out. Once the ball is in play, any ball that strikes a partner is deemed a side out or a loss of point, depending on whether the serving or receiving team committed the infraction. The receiving team must stand behind the imaginary five-foot line to receive serve. Hinders are the same as in singles play, but the possibility for hinder calls is magnified by the presence of four players on the court at one time.

The cut throat game is an unofficial racquetball game with a safety feature built in. One cut throat game is a two-against-one setup, with the receiving team playing as a doubles team, and the serving player competing against that team. Following each side out, the doubles team membership changes, and the server becomes a part of a new doubles team. All play on the part of the doubles team as related to movement and position utilizes doubles rules, and all other play commences as in singles. The serving rotation follows a sequence of the server as the number-one player exchanging with the number-two player, who is a receiver. When the next side out occurs, the number-two player, who has been the server, exchanges with the number-three player, who is the second receiver. The sequence follows an exchange with the number-three player (who is the server) on the next side out with the number-one player, who has moved through the sequence as receiver. Then the process is repeated. It should be noted that this type of exchange alternates the position of the receiver each time through the full serving sequence. If the number-two receiver started from a right-side receiving position during the first sequence, that number-two player would receive from the left side during the second sequence of return of serve.

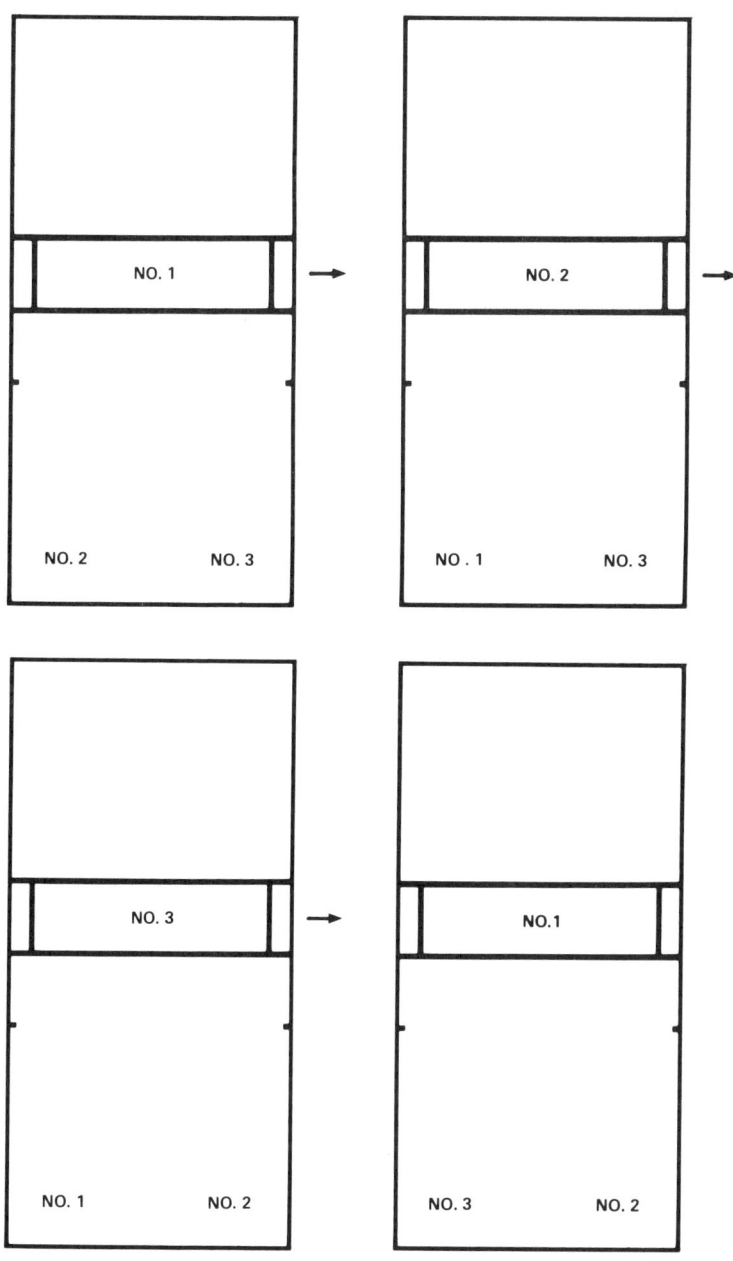

Cut throat rotation

The second type of cut throat game is a safer version and becomes a singles match with three players. One player is always sitting out a particular point by standing in a back-wall area, while the other two players are playing. At the conclusion of each point, the non-competing player enters the game as a receiver of the serve, and the player who lost the point steps out. If the server loses the point, the former receiver becomes the server. If the receiver loses the point, the server remains as server, and play continues. In both games of cut throat, each player keeps an individual score, and the winner is the first player to gain 21 points. The game of cut throat provides for a change-of-pace situation that permits three people to enjoy a game designed for two or four.

Chapter Thirteen

Resources In Racquetball

Resources in racquetball include information regarding organizations and associations. Then there are the human resources — usually college racquetball instructors and teaching professionals associated with racquetball clubs. Racquetball publications are a third source of information that will provide instructional and strategy data. A novice racquetball player needs insight on how to get started in racquetball competition, including information on the types of tournaments available, the difference between competitive and recreational play, and the playing level at which a player should begin to compete.

Information For The Racquetball Player

There is only one *racquetball association* presently devoted to amateur racquetball participation — the AMERICAN AMATEUR RACQUETBALL ASSOCIATION (AARA). One of the AARA's responsibilities is to take a grass-roots approach to racquetball, beginning with junior programs and progressing through the master's level. Intercollegiate racquetball through national intercollegiate tournaments is a grass-roots program sponsored by the AARA. The U.S. Collegiate Championships completed their eleventh year of tournament play for collegians in Memphis, Tennessee, in 1983. At that tournament, 44 universities were represented with 6 full 8-player teams fielded from the total participants. The 8-player teams consisted of 4 men and 4 women with a #1 and #2 singles for both men and women and a doubles competition for each. A total of $8,000 in scholarships was awarded at the Memphis tournament for first, second, and third place finishers.

The AARA sanctions more than 800 tournaments per year, maintains a uniform racquetball rules book, and sponsors the numerous regional and state racquetball associations. The AARA is devoted to the development of racquetball as an international sport, and it works toward the inclusion of racquetball as an Olympic sport. Since 1969, numerous changes have occurred in the leadership of racquetball in the United States. When the AARA assumed the American leadership role and moved to Colorado Springs, Colorado, it became associated with the United States Olympic Committee (USOC) as a national governing body. That affiliation has provided a credibility of leadership in amateur racquetball that is beginning to establish a stability in the sport.

The AARA publishes the newsletter *In Review*, which is the official publication for the association. Members of AARA receive the newsletter 9 times per year. The association also promotes racquetball through the military groups (Air Force, Navy, and Marine Corps). It sponsors racquetball for the disabled and for wheelchair participants. The AARA promotes the game internationally through the INTERNATIONAL AMATEUR RACQUETBALL ASSOCIATION (IARA), and the numerous foreign associations, including those in Japan, Thailand, the Philippines, the Republic of China, Hong Kong, Australia, and North America.

Membership in the AARA at present costs only $6.00 and can be acquired by writing Luke St. Onge, Executive Director. American Amateur Racquetball Association, 815 N. Weber, Suite 203, Colorado Springs, Colorado 80903. Membership for an aspiring racquetball player will permit him/her to support amateur racquetball, be informed on tournament dates, receive *In Review*, and be kept up-to-date on the most recent rules adoptions.

Another racquetball resource is *National Racquetball*, a national periodical (1800 Pickwick Ave., Glenview, Illinois 60025). *National Racquetball* is described as the authoritative voice of the sport. It contains 16 instructional pages per issue, information on new products, health tips, tournament results, and information on new events. An international publication, *International Racquetball* also promotes racquetball in many parts of the world. State organizations often publish a newsletter for local state interest. In Colorado, for example, the publication is entitled *Rollout*, and it provides information on racquetball for state members. A national newsletter, *Racquetball Today*, is published by a private enterprise and includes information on instruction and playing techniques, tournament news, humor, and health.

Corporations also promote racquetball. Ektelon produces racquets and racquetball accessories. It sponsors tournaments and publishes instructional booklets that include information on skill acquisition and strategy. Ektelon is just one company that promotes racquetball through equipment, tournaments, and instructional publications. Among the many corporations affiliated with racquetball are 3 presently identified with the AARA as sponsors of AARA-sanctioned tournaments. These three companies are D. P. Leach (Diversified Products Corporation), Penn Racquetball (Penn Athletic Products Co.), and Miller Lite Beer. Each corporation furnishes prizes for sanctioned tournaments and promotes racquetball both in tournament settings and generally throughout the country.

There are vast *human resources* available to developing racquetball players. Every college and/or university has a plethora of racquetball instructors who are knowledgeable and willing to help a player improve. There are also numerous club professionals who have competed at the amateur or professional level and earn their living giving lessons. Community and private recreation centers have qualified instructors who will teach racquetball to small groups. As with all instructional situations, some racquetball instructors will be more capable than others, and when you seek instructional help, you should ask questions of the teacher, including:

1. How much individual time will you give me? (The more the better.)
2. Who are some of your previous students? (Once you have the names, go ahead and contact them for their opinion of the instructor.)
3. What will you teach me? (You need to develop as a player rather than repeat past learning experiences.)

Asking questions of an instructor provides insight as to what to expect during instruction. A secure instructor will willingly volunteer answers to the questions listed above, and he/she will be pleased to provide you with additional information. One other human resource is the person with whom you practice. If you play individuals more skilled and knowledgeable than you, or at least a player of equal skill and knowledge, your racquetball skills will continue to improve.

How to Get Started in Racquetball Competition

The aspiring racquetball player must understand that once skill development progresses to the point of being able to play with success in practice matches and friendly play, he/she may want to play more competitively. Not all players need to play competitively by participating in tournaments, and many are quite satisfied to continue in a totally recreational environment. For individuals who enjoy competition with pressure, and for those who want to develop a tournament-hardened competitive edge, tournament play becomes a requirement.

Every college/university campus with racquetball courts has an *intramural or campus recreation program* that will sponsor 2 or 3 tournaments per academic year. These tournaments are excellent first experiences for players who want to play in a tournament. The majority of players who participate in these tournaments are novices who move from a racquetball instructional class to their first tournament. Comparable tournaments in a community are found in *community recreation programs.* These tournaments also provide an opportunity for a first-time experience. A racquetball player can enter a tournament at a variety of levels, ranging from a novice rating through D, C, B, and A categories. Usually when a player wins at a certain level, he/she must move up to the next category for further tournament play.

Competitive versus recreational tournament play choice is contingent on how serious you are about practice and about extending the effort to develop as a player. Many players are comfortable with tournament play at a campus or community recreation level. Others may want to progress to another level of competition usually identified with club tournaments sanctioned by state racquetball associations and/or the AARA. These tournaments typically provide numerous levels of play. Categories are varied in these tournaments, but representative examples are identified in Table 13.1.

Another high level of competition, at least for men and women at the *collegiate level,* is the U.S. Collegiate Championships mentioned earlier. There are also state collegiate racquetball championships sponsored in many states.

The most sophisticated level of tournament racquetball is the *professional tournament play,* which is well beyond the scope of this text in terms of skill acquisition. Only a rare few men and women reach this level of play. For the aspiring player with high-quality skills and experience, the professional playing circuit is a possibility, but the degree of effort required to achieve at that level is massive. All racquetball players should at least be encouraged to view a

Table 13.1
EXAMPLES OF PLAYING CATEGORIES
IN SANCTIONED RACQUETBALL TOURNAMENTS

NATIONAL LEVEL	LOCAL LEVEL #1	LOCAL LEVEL #2
Open	Open Singles	Open Singles
Junior Vets 25+	A Singles	A Singles
Senior 30+	B Singles	B Singles
Senior 35+	C Singles	CC Singles
Senior 40+	Novice Singles	D Singles
Master 45+	A Doubles	30+ Singles
Master 50+	B Doubles	35+ Singles
Grand Master 55+	C Doubles	40+ Singles
Grand Master 60+	Mixed A Doubles	50+ Singles
Grand Master 65+	Mixed B Doubles	A Doubles
	Mixed C Doubles	B Doubles
		CC Doubles
		D Doubles
		30+ Doubles
		35+ Doubles
		40+ Doubles
		50+ Doubles

professional tournament to better understand the high level of skill required to excel at this degree of play. Observation at the professional level continually provides a learning experience and serves as yet another resource.

Chapter Fourteen

The Foundations of Racquetball

Racquetball is a relatively new game in the form in which Americans are now playing it. A player new to the game should be aware of the recent history of the game and understand the sociological perspectives associated with racquetball.

Recent Events That Have Increased Racquetball Participation

Racquetball has developed from numerous games into an identity all its own. The strokes, strategy, and play concepts came from two racquet sports — paddleball and squash — and a court game — handball. Paddleball was initially played with a wooden paddle, and it evolved from a combination of the games of tennis and handball. The popularity of paddleball grew slowly from the 1920s to the 1960s, and sports technology in the form of the development of a new racquet with strings, led to the beginnings of racquetball. Handball also played a major role in the development of racquetball through the early years, sharing the same type of court and promoting the sport through the handball magazine and the United States Handball Association. The game of squash provided further incentive for racquetball by utilizing the same concepts of court play as in handball, and by implying that a game played with a wider striking surface and a shorter racquet handle might permit more individuals to gain skill in a reasonably quick time. This encouraged a transition from squash to racquetball. The evolution of racquetball occurred through squash, paddleball, handball, and, in an associated manner, through tennis. Handball perhaps played the greatest role by promoting racquetball and by switching several handball players to the new game.

The association of racquetball and handball was short-lived. Handball players began to complain bitterly that the racquetball enthusiast was taking over the handball courts. As a result, racquetball leaders in 1973 developed their own organization called the National Racquetball Club, which sponsored a professional tour of racquetball players and an amateur organization called the United States Racquetball Association, an offshoot of the National Racquetball Club. Both organizations helped to make racquetball a highly visible sport to the point that new sporting clubs with numerous racquetball courts began emerging throughout the country, providing enough courts for both racquetball and handball players. The visibility of the professional tour encouraged players to continue to develop their skills and pulled sport participants from tennis and handball to the game. The game emerged as an exciting activity in which people of all skill levels could participate, and it became a game that both sexes could find highly satisfying as opposed to handball, which was basically male-dominated. From the first national championship of 1969 to the present day, there has been a fantastic growth of the sport that promises to continue into the turn of the century.

The Sociological Perspective of Racquetball in the United States

The concept that sport is a microcosm of society pertains to racquetball — it represents American society. Of the various social aspects related to sport and society, economics is perhaps the most noteworthy. The "American way" is a free enterprise system of government and economics. The economic growth of racquetball has developed by great strides. The sporting houses or sports clubs that have emerged with numerous racquetball courts have developed under the theory of supply and demand. Very few racquetball courts existed in the 1970s, and those that there were had been designed for handball enthusiasts. The number of courts did not meet the demand by the ever-growing population, which began to request adequate facilities. The entrepreneurs who had the foresight to build courts were in the lead economically, thus encouraging even more participation. Colleges and universities have not been able to keep up with the demand, and, of course, the secondary school physical education facilities in this area have been practically nonexistent.

Recent developments in the technical aspects of racquetball courts have included the use of prefabricated, hard, 4' x 8' wall surfaces butted together. These provide for a non-mar surface and for a more even bounce of the ball. Other advances include the use of lighting, such as mercury vapor illumination, and the use of glass walls. Technical development has insured a new business expertise in the area of building racquetball courts, and this has been an economic boon.

Racquetball equipment has proliferated through the advent of the game's popularity. Numerous racquet manufacturers have designed racquets composed of light material, including aluminum, fiberglass, graphite, and composition materials that include wood. They provide flexibility, balance, and lightweight maneuverability. The racquets have been designed to make money for the innovating corporation and to encourage the player to purchase the latest design. Racquetball accessories have also become a necessity for players. These items include shirts, shorts, warm-up suits, glasses, equipment bags, and gloves. As you can see, a simple game called racquetball, which evolved from paddleball via handball and squash, has developed into a multi-million-dollar business. Even individuals who play only a small amount of racquetball enjoy dressing and looking the part.

Racquetball has even become something of a "pseudo-religious" sport. Players participate in the game much as they would participate in a religious experience. A form of tithing is represented by the dues that a member of a club must pay each month. The amount of time spent in playing the game, volunteering to work with youngsters who are learning the game, assisting in tournaments as assistant directors and officials, and attending social functions is representative of what happens in some church situations. Just as religious bodies have sacraments, special holidays, ceremonies, and rituals, racquetball participants who follow the rules to the letter have days for special tournaments. These players go through rituals in preparing for the game, including prayer and certain repetitive steps that they think will bring them good luck.

Racquetball also has its idols, its proverbs, and its emotional attachments. There are missionaries who communicate their beliefs to individuals throughout the world, and there are racquetball missionaries who continually espouse the virtues of the game. The puritan work ethic is highly endorsed by the majority of American churches, and that ethic surfaces in the effort to practice and achieve success in playing the game of racquetball. This analogy is in no way intended to belittle religion, but rather to demonstrate the seriousness assumed by racquetball participants.

The behavior of the racquetball player is in some ways representative of the behavior of individuals in society at large. There is an inner glow (and sometimes an outer glow) associated with winning in racquetball. The same satisfaction exists with a person who receives a raise, passes an exam in a college course, or receives an award for something well done. Losing causes a multitude of reactions, including acceptance, being upset, and not caring. In society, the same reaction occurs when an individual is faced with defeat in life.

The recent growth of racquetball can be attributed to the nature of American people. If people find something that they like, they will do it and serve as enthusiastic promoters of that activity. So it is in racquetball when individuals find a sport that they can enjoy and play reasonably well. The media, which often has a major impact on the growth of a sport, has yet to impact racquetball directly through television. The media storm has occurred through the various racquetball magazines that materialized on the racks of the typical bookstore. If television were ever to market the game based on fan or spectator viewing, racquetball would probably become doubly popular.

Glossary of Terms in Racquetball

Ace: A legal serve that is totally missed by the receiver of the serve.

Anxiety: The act of being anxious, thus creating a tension in the muscle groups that subsequently impairs performance.

Around-the-wall Ball: A shot that strikes 3 walls before hitting the floor.

Avoidable Hinder: An intentional interference with the opponent's opportunity to play a shot fairly.

Back Court: That section of the court nearest the back wall and described as the last third of the court.

Backhand: A stroke hit from the non-racquet side of the body.

Backswing: The preparation phase of the basic swing.

Ceiling Shot: A ball that strikes ceiling-front wall or front wall-ceiling in sequence.

Center Court: The area immediately behind the short-line and equal distance from the side walls.

Closed Face: Position of the racquet face on the ball when hitting the ball downward.

Competition: The act of participating in a game situation with the concept that the opponent is secondary to the barrier that the opponent presents through shot making and strategy.

Continental Grip: The grip positioned halfway between the eastern forehand and backhand grip.

Corner Kill Shot: The kill shot that strikes the front wall-side wall and rebounds in the direction of the mid court.

Cross-Court Passing Shot: A two-wall passing shot executed when the opponent is either on the same side as you or is in an "up" position. The ball hits front wall and then side wall.

Crotch: A ball that strikes 2 playing surfaces simultaneously.

Cut Throat: A 3-player racquetball game designed with the server playing against the other 2 players.
Defensive shots: Shots that prevent the opponent from holding an offensive court position.
Doubles: A 4-player racquetball game played between teams of 2 players.
Down-the-line Passing Shot: A shot that carries along a side wall 1 to 2′ from the wall and below the opponent's waist. This is also called down-the-wall, and it is designed to pass an opponent who is in an "up" position.
Drop Shot: A touch shot that is hit with deception and little force.
Eastern Forehand Grip: The conventional racquetball grip that is best described as a "shake hands" position.
Eastern Backhand Grip: The conventional backhand grip that is assumed by rotating the racquet a quarter turn to the racquet side of the body.
Fault: A serve that touches the floor before passing the short line or one in which the ball strikes the front wall and either the ceiling, the back wall, or 2 side walls before hitting the floor. These serves are illegal and must be replayed. Two faults result in a side out.
Flow: The intangible feeling of being in tune with the environment and reacting instinctively without thinking.
Forehand: A stroke hit from the racquet side of the body.
Front Court: That section of the court in front of the service court line.
Front Wall Kill: The kill shot that hits the front wall straight on and rebounds toward the back wall without touching a side wall.
Garbage Serve: A serve hit in between the speed of a drive and lob serve that bounces between shoulder and waist to the receiver. The serve gives an illusion of a miss-hit serve.
Goggles: Safety glasses required for wear when entering a racquetball court.
High Z Serve: A serve that strikes high off the front wall (near the ceiling) and follows a "Z" pattern across the court.
Hinder: Any situation that prevents an opponent from having a fair shot at hitting the ball during a rally. Hinders include avoidable, unavoidable, and court hinders.
Kill Shot: Any ball that strikes the front wall hard and low so that the rebound with the floor occurs almost simultaneously with the wall. A winning offensive shot.

Lob: A defensive shot, hit along a side wall so that it follows a path high over center court and falls with little rebound into a back corner. This ball may touch a side wall close to the back corner.

Long: A serve that strikes the back wall on the fly. A fault.

Match: The culmination of a competition with the winner usually winning 2 of 3 games.

Mental Rehearsal: The mental preparation of a player through a simulated vision of play. Playing out skills and game strategy through an image process.

Mid Court: The area between the service and short line and the two side walls.

Non-Thinking Strategy: Following a defensive reactive strategy with few decisions to make.

Offensive Shot: The attempt to win a point outright by virtue of the skill with which the shot is hit.

"On Edge": The position of the racquet face perpendicular to the floor.

Open Face: Position of the racquet face on the ball when hitting the ball up.

Overhead: Shots hit from above the shoulder position with an extended arm.

Overhead Kill: A kill shot hit from above the shoulder position.

Over-the-Shoulder: A ball hit from a position directly over the shoulder.

Passing Shot: An offensive shot that literally goes past an opponent who is in the front-, mid-, or center-court positions.

Pendulum Swing: A scooping swing used to hit balls high off the front wall or to the ceiling.

Pinch Kill: A shot that strikes the side wall-front wall sequence and that is unreturnable due to the low, high velocity of the shot. Also called a pinch shot.

Racquet Face: The portion of the racquet with which the ball is struck during play.

Rally: A continuous exchange of shots during the play of a point.

Receiving Line: The line identified by the vertical, side wall marks located 5 feet behind the short line.

"Run the Corner": A ball that rebounds to a back corner, hitting the side wall and back wall before striking floor.

Safety Hinder: A hinder called to prevent an injury.

Screen: A blocking of the opponent's vision, preventing the opponent from seeing the ball.

Service Line: The line on the floor closest to the front wall. The front line of the service zone.

Service Zone: The area between the service line and the short line. The position for the server to legally execute the serve.

Set: The ready position. The position that enables the receiver of a shot to turn or pivot to hit the ball.

Set Up: A ball that is hit so that the opponent can easily return it.

Short: A ball that does not clear the short line on the fly. A fault.

Short Line: The line on the floor nearest the back wall. The back line of the service zone.

Side Out: A loss of a serve to the opponent.

Skip Ball: A ball that strikes the floor before hitting the front wall.

Thong: The safety strap that is attached to the racquet grip and worn around the wrist.

Thinking Strategy: The act of taking advantage of an opponent through the use of intellect, court strategy, and skill.

Three-Wall Shot: A defensive shot that rebounds off 3 walls.

Unavoidable Hinder: An unintentional interference with the opponent's opportunity to play a shot fairly.

Volley: Striking the ball in midair from a rebound off the front wall.

Wallpaper Shot: A shot that lies against the side wall, making a return extremely difficult.

Western Grip: The grip that is assumed for a forehand grip when the racquet is picked up off the floor.

The Aspiring Racquetball Player's Self-Appraisal Checklist

If a racquetball student is receiving instruction, the teacher provides feedback on skill development. Once you begin to play independent of instruction, the feedback is reduced considerably. The self-appraisal checklist for the racquetball player is designed to fill the void of minimal feedback. It lists skills that the player should have acquired and provides a percentage breakdown of progress in skill development.

The skills are divided into strategy skills, mental relaxation skills, and physical playing skills. For each skill, you need to determine which of the 5 percentage categories best reflects the level of your skill development.

If you classify your play, strategy, and relaxation skills at 90 percent and above proficiency, then you would check that box. The 90 percent level for play skill is defined (as described in Chapter 11) as an excellent "bread and butter" shot that will be successfully executed nearly every time it is attempted. The practice of mental relaxation at the 90 percent level indicates that relaxation is almost always a major contributing factor associated with performance. Strategy skills that are identified with the 90 percent level are indicative of nearly flawless planning and extensive contribution to the play results.

A 75 to 84 percent assessment of performance in the 3 areas is representative of consistent performance. This success rate is better than 3 out of 4 attempts meeting with success. That level of playing success is excellent when you are still developing skills in stroke execution. A 50 percent plus evaluation of performance in physical, relaxation, and strategy skills indicates that success only occurs half the time. This self-evaluation of performance implies that a void exists in the 3 areas that can be remedied by intensive practice and motivation to improve. If you evaluate yourself at the 25 percent plus level, you have only minimal ability to execute the skills associated with playing success. Only extensive practice over a long period of time will raise your level of play. Strategy skills rated in the 25 to 49 percent category should be eliminated from your repertoire of shots executed in play until they are refined in practice. An assessment of 0 to 24 percent means a lack of skill to meet even minimal skill requirements. This type of self-rating means that you cannot execute the skill and that you do not comprehend what is expected to acquire the skill.

A player who assesses physical, strategy, and relaxation skills at a 75 or 90 percent plus level is well on the way to becoming a capable racquetball player. Those players who self-assess below the 75 percent plus level must recognize their need for practice and continued effort.

The Racquetball Player's Self-Appraisal Checklist

Strategy Skills:	90%+	75%+	50%+	25%+	0%+
Understands the strategy of assuming control of the front court					
Understands when to hit a defensive shot					
Understands when to hit an offensive shot					
Can comprehend the placement of the ball using the various angles of the wall, and can position accordingly					
Can use the angles of the court walls to a strategic advantage					
Can execute a defensive shot when required to do so under pressure ..					
Can execute an offensive shot when required to do so under pressure ..					
Mental Relaxation Skills:					
Comprehends the concept of playing relaxed................					
Comprehends the use of and practices muscle tension recognition and relaxation.........					
Capable of using the appropriate attentional focus..................					
Has eliminated negative thoughts and responses during play					
Can feel the "flow" during play					
Recognizes when anxiety is contributing to poor play, and is able to change the stress level.....					
Blocks out an opponent's behavior that is detrimental to positive play experiences..........					
Understands the real meaning of competition					
Physical Playing Skills:					
Can hit a ceiling — front wall shot					
Can hit a front wall — ceiling shot					

The Racquetball Player's Self-Appraisal Checklist (Cont.)

Physical Playing Skills (Cont.):	90%+	75%+	50%+	25%+	0%+
Can hit a pinch shot; right corner					
Can hit a pinch shot; left corner					
Can hit a straight kill					
Can hit a one-wall passing shot					
Can hit a two-wall passing shot (cross-court)					
Can hit off the back wall in timing with the ball					
Can hit a drop shot					
Can hit a Z shot as a defensive shot					
Can hit high Z serves					
Can hit low Z serves					
Can hit a drive serve					
Can hit a lob serve					
Can hit serves with a variation of speeds					
Can hit a cross-court drive return of serve					
Can hit a down-the-line return of serve					
Can hit a kill return of serve					
Can hit a ceiling return of serve					
Can hit an around-the-wall return of serve					
Can hit volley shots effectively (ceiling, pinch, kill, drives, etc.)					
Can execute with sound form the basic forehand					
Can execute with sound form the basic backhand					

Official American Amateur Racquetball Association Rules

1 — THE GAME

A. TYPES OF GAMES
Racquetball may be played by two, three, or four players. When played by two it is called "singles", when played by three, "cut throat", and when played by four, "doubles".

B. DESCRIPTION
Racquetball, as the name implies, is a competitive game in which only one racquet is used by each player to serve and return the ball.

C. OBJECTIVE
The objective is to win each rally by serving or returning the ball so the opponent is unable to keep the ball in play. A rally is over when a side makes an error, or is unable to return the ball before it touches the floor twice, or if a hinder is called.

D. POINTS AND OUTS
Points are scored only by the server/(serving team) when it serves an ace or wins a rally. When the serving side loses a rally, it loses the serve. Losing the serve is called an "out" in singles, and a "handout", or "side out" in doubles.

E. GAME
A game is won by the side first scoring 21 points (or 11 points in the tiebreaker). A player need only win by one point.

F. MATCH
A match is won by the first side winning two games. The first two games of a match are played to 21 points, and the tie-breaker to 11 points. (Games may be won by one point.) In the event that each participant or team wins one game, the match shall be decided by an eleven (11) point tiebreaker.

G. DOUBLES TEAM
A doubles team shall consist of two players that meet either/or the age requirements or player classification requirements to participate in a particular division of play. A team must be classified by the ability level (or player classification) of the higher ranked player on the team.

A change in playing partners may not be made after the final draw has been made and posted. Under no circumstances can a partner change be made during the course of a tournament without the consent of the Tournament Director.

H. CONSOLATION MATCHES
1) Consolation matches may be waived at the discretion of the Tournament Director, but this waiver must be in writing on the tournament application.
2) In all AARA Sanctioned tournaments each entrant shall be entitled to participate in a minimum of two matches. This then means that losers of their first match shall have the opportunity to compete in a consolation bracket of their own division. In draws of less than seven (7) players, a round-robin format may be offered.

2 — COURTS AND EQUIPMENT

A. COURTS
The specifications for the standard four wall racquetball court are:
1) **Dimension.** The dimensions shall be 20 feet wide, 20 feet high, and 40 feet long, with a back wall at least 12 feet high. All surfaces within the court shall be deemed "in play" with the exception of any gallery openings or surfaces designated as "court-hinders."
2) **Lines and Zones.** Racquetball courts shall be divided and marked with 1½ inch wide lines as follows:
   a) Short Line. The back edge of the short line is midway between (20') and parallel to the front and back walls, thus dividing the court into equal front and back courts.
   b) Service Line. The front edge of the service line is parallel with and

located five feet in front of the back edge of the short line.
c) Service Zone. The service zone is the area between the outer edges of the short and service lines.
d) Service Boxes. The service boxes are located at each end of the service zone and designated by lines parallel with each side wall. The inside edge of the lines are 18 inches from the side walls.
e) Receiving Lines. Five feet back of the short line, vertical lines shall be marked on each side wall extending 3 to 6 inches from the floor. The back edge of the receiving lines shall be five feet from the back edge of the short line.

B. BALL SPECIFICATIONS
1) The standard racquetball shall be 2¼" in diameter; weigh approximately 1.4 ounces, and at a temperature of 70-74 °F., with a 100 inch drop rebound is to be 68-72 inches; hardness, 55-60 inches durometer.
2) Any ball which carries the endorsement stamp of approval from the AARA is an official ball. Only AARA approved balls may be used in AARA sanctioned tournaments.

C. BALL SELECTION
1) A ball shall be selected by referee for use in each match. During the match the referee either at his discretion, or at the request of a player or team, may replace the game ball. Balls that are not round or which bounce erratically shall not be used.
2) In tournament play, the referee and the players shall agree to an alternate ball, so that in the event of breakage, the second ball can be put into play immediately.

D. RACQUET SPECIFICATIONS
1) **Dimensions.** The total sum of the length and width of the racquet may not exceed 27 inches. The length of the head, measured from the top of the handle to the top of the head, may not exceed 13.5 inches. The head width may not exceed 9 inches. These measurements are computed from the outer edge of the racquet head rims. The handle may not exceed 7 inches in length.
2) The regulation racquet frame may be of any material, as long as it conforms to the above specifications.
3) The regulation racquet must include a thong that must be securely attached to the player's wrist.

4) The string of the racquet should be gut, monofilament, nylon, graphite, plastic, metal, or a combination thereof, providing strings do not mark or deface the ball.

E. UNIFORM
1) The uniform and shoes may be of any color but must have soles which do not mark or damage the court floor. The shirt may contain any insignia or writing considered in good taste by the Tournament Director. Players are required to wear shirts. Extremely loose fitting or otherwise distracting garments are not permissible.
2) Eye protection is required for any participant under the age of 19 in *all* AARA sanctioned tournaments.

3 — OFFICIATING AND PLAY REGULATIONS

Rule 1. A. TOURNAMENTS
All tournaments shall be managed by a committee or Tournament Director who shall designate the officials.

Rule 1. B. OFFICIALS
The official shall be a referee designated by the tournament director or the floor manager or one agreed to by both participants (teams in doubles). Officials may also include, at the discretion of the tournament director, a scorekeeper and two linespeople.

Rule 1. C. REMOVAL OF REFEREE
A referee may be removed upon the agreement of both participants (teams in doubles) or at the discretion of the tournament director or rules officials. In the event that a referee's removal is requested by one player (team) and not agreed to by the other, the tournament director or officials may accept or reject the request.

Rule 1. D. RULE BRIEFING
Before all tournaments, all officials and players shall be briefed on rules and on court hinders or regulations or modifications the tournament director wishes to impose. This briefing should be reduced to writing. The current AARA rules will apply and be made available. Any modifications the tournament director wishes to impose must be stated on the entry form and in writing and be available to all players at registration.

Rule 1. E. REFEREES
1) **Pre-match Duties.** Before each match begins, it shall be the duty of the referee to:
   a) Check on adequacy of preparation of court with respect to cleanliness, lighting, and temperature.

b) Check on availability and suitability of materials necessary for the match such as balls, towels, score cards, pencils, and time piece.
c) Instruct players on court.
d) Point court hinders and local regulations.
e) Inspect equipment and toss coin.
f) Check linespeople and score keeper and ask for reserve game ball upon assuming officiating position.
g) Review any rule modifications in effect for this particular tournament.

2) **Decisions.** During the match, the referee shall make all decisions with regard to the rules. Where linespeople are used, the referee shall announce all final judgments. If both players in singles and three out of four in a doubles match disagree with a judgment call made by the referee, the referee is overruled. The referee shall have jurisdiction over the spectators as well as players while the match is in progress.

3) **Protests.** Any decision not involving the judgment of the referee may, on protest, be decided by the tournament director or designated official.

4) **Forfeitures.** A match may be forfeited by the referee when:
a) Any player refuses to abide by the referee's decision, or engages in unsportsmanlike conduct.
b) A player or team may be forfeited by the tournament director or official for failure to comply with the tournament or host facility's rules while on the premises, for failure to referee, for improper conduct on the premises between matches, or for abuse of hospitality, locker room or other rules and procedures.
c) Any player or team fails to report to play ten (10) minutes after the match has been called to play. (The tournament director may permit a longer delay if circumstances warrant such a decision.)

Rule 1. F. 1) LINESPEOPLE

Two linespeople are recommended for all matches from the semifinals on up, subject to availability and subject to the discretion of the tournament officials. The linespeople shall be selected by the officials and situated as designated by the officials. If any player objects to the selection of a linesperson before the match begins, all reasonable effort shall be made to find a replacement acceptable to the officials and players. If a player or team objects to a linesperson after the match begins, replacement shall be under the discretion of the referee and officials.

Rule 1. F. 2)

Linespeople are designated in order to help decide appealed rulings. Two linespeople will be designated by the referee and shall, at the referee's signal, either agree or disagree with the referee's ruling. The signal by a linesperson to show agreement with the referee is "thumb up." The signal to show disagreement is "thumb down." The signal for no opinion is "open palm down." If both linespeople signal no opinion, the referee's call stands. If both linespeople disagree with the referee, the referee must reverse the ruling. If one linesperson agrees and one disagrees or has no opinion, the referee's call shall stand. If one linesperson disagrees and one has no opinion, the rally or serve shall be replayed. Any replays will result in two serves with the exception of appeals on the second serve itself.

Rule 1. G. APPEALS

In any match using linespeople a player or team may appeal only the following calls made (or failed to be made) by the referee:

1) **Kill Shot Appeals.** If the referee makes a call of: "good" on a kill shot attempt which ends a particular rally, the loser of the rally may appeal the call. If the appeal is successful and the referee's original call reversed, the side which originally lost the rally is declared the winner of the rally. If the referee makes a call of "bad" or "skip" on a kill shot attempt, the rally has ended and the side against whom the call was made has the right to appeal the call if they felt the shot was good. If the appeal is successful and the referee's original call reversed, the referee must then decide if the shot could have been returned had play continued. If the shot could have been (or was) returned, the rally shall be replayed. If the shot was a kill or pass that the opponent could not have retrieved (in the referee's opinion), the side which originally lost the rally is declared the winner of the rally. The referee's judgment in this matter is final. Any rally replayed shall afford the server two serves.

2) **Fault Serve Appeals.** If the referee makes a call of "fault" on a serve, the server may appeal the call. If the appeal is successful, the server is entitled to replay the serve. If the served ball was considered by the referee to be an ace, then a point shall be awarded to the server. If the referee makes "no call" on a serve (therefore indicating that the serve was "good"), either side may appeal, then the situation reverts to the point of service with the call becoming fault. If it was a first service, one more serve is allowed. If the serve was a second serve, then the fault serve would cause an out.

3) **Out Serve Appeals.** If the referee makes a call of "out serve" thereby stopping the play, the serving side may appeal the call. If the appeal is successful, the referee shall revise the call to the proper call and the service shall be replayed or a point awarded if the resulting serve was an ace. If the referee makes "no call", or calls a "fault" serve, and the receiver feels it was an "out" serve, the receiver may appeal. If the appeal is successful the service results in an "out".

4) **Double Bounce Pickup Appeals.** If the referee makes a call of "two bounces", thereby stopping play, the side against whom the call was made has the right of appeal. If the appeal is upheld, the rally is replayed or the referee may award the rally to the hitter if the resulting shot could not have been retrieved by the opponent (and providing the referee's call did not cause the opponent to hesitate or stop play). If the referee makes "no call" on a particular play, indicating thereby that the player hit the ball before the second bounce, the opponent has the right to appeal at the end of the rally. However, since the ball is in play, the side wishing to appeal must clearly motion to the referee and linespeople by raising their non-racquet hand, thereby alerting the officials as to the exact shot which is being appealed. At the same time, the player appealing must continue to play. If the appealing player should lose the rally, and the appeal is upheld, the player who appealed then becomes the winner of the rally. All rallies replayed as the result of a double bounce pickup appeal shall result in the server getting two serves.

Rules Interpretations. If a player feels that the referee has interpreted the rules incorrectly, they may require the referee or tournament director to show them the applicable rule in the rule book.

RULE 2. SERVE
Rule 2. A. ORDER

The player or side winning the toss becomes the first server and starts the first game. The loser of the toss will serve first in the second game. The player or team scoring the most total points in games one and two shall serve first in the tie-breaker. In the event that both players or teams score an equal number of points in the first two games, another coin toss shall determine the server in the tie-breaker.

Rule 2. B. START

The serve is started from any place within the service zone. No part of either foot may extend beyond either line of the service zone. Stepping on, but not over the line is permitted. The server must remain in the service zone from the moment the service motion begins until the served ball passes the short line. Violations are called "foot faults". The server may not start any service motion until the referee has called the score or second serve.

Rule 2. C. MANNER

The serve is commenced by bouncing the ball to the floor while standing within the confines of the service zone and is struck by the server's racquet so that the ball hits the front wall first and on rebound hits the floor behind the back edge of the short line, either with or without touching one of the side walls. A balk serve or fake swing at the ball shall be deemed an infraction and be judged an "out" "handout", or "side out."

Rule 2. D. READINESS

Serves shall not be made until the receiving side is ready and the referee has called the score. The referee shall call the score as both server and receiver prepare to return to their respective position, shortly after the previous point has ended.

Rule 2. E. DELAYS

Delays on the part of the server or receiver exceeding 10 seconds shall result in an out or point against the offender.

1) This "10 second rule" is applicable to both server and receiver, each of whom is allowed up to 10 seconds after the score is called, to serve or be ready to receive. It is the server's responsibility to look and be certain that the receiver is ready. If the receiver is not ready, they must signal so by either raising their racquet above their head or completely turning their back to the server (these are the only two acceptable signals).

2) If the server serves the ball while the receiver is signaling "not ready", the

serve shall go over with no penalty and the server shall be "warned" by the referee to check the receiver. If the server continues to serve without checking the receiver, the referee may award a "technical" for delay of game.

3) After the score is called, if the server looks at the receiver and the receiver is not signalling "not ready", the server may then serve. If the receiver attempts to signal "not ready" after that point, such signal shall not be acknowledged and the serve becomes legal.

RULE 3. SERVE IN DOUBLES
Rule 3. A. SERVER
At the beginning of each game in doubles, each side shall inform the referee of the order of service which shall be followed throughout the game. When the first server is out the first time up, the side is out. Thereafter, both players on each side shall serve until each receive a hand-out.

Rule 3. B. PARTNER'S POSITION
On each serve the server's partner shall stand erect with back to the sidewall and with both feet on the floor within the service box from the moment the server begins his service motion until the served ball passes the short line. Violations are called "foot faults".

RULE 4. DEFECTIVE SERVES
Defective serves are of three types resulting in penalties as follows:

Rule 4. A. DEAD BALL SERVE
A dead ball serve results in no penalty and the server is given another serve (without cancelling a prior illegal serve).

Rule 4. B. FAULT SERVE
Two (2) fault serves results in a handout.

Rule 4. C. OUT SERVE
An out serve results in a hand out.

RULE 5. DEAD BALL SERVES
Dead ball serves do not cancel any previous illegal serve. They occur when an otherwise legal serve:

Rule 5. A. HITS PARTNER
Hits the server's partner on the fly on the rebound from the front wall while the server's partner is in the service box. Any serve that touches the floor before hitting the partner in the box is short.

Rule 5. B. SCREEN BALLS
Passes so close to the server or server's partner as to obstruct the view of the returning side. Any serve passing behind the server's partner and the side wall is an automatic screen.

Rule 5. C. COURT HINDERS
Hits any part of the court that under local rules is a dead ball.

Rule 5. D. BROKEN BALL
If the ball is determined to have broken on the serve, a new ball shall be substituted and the serve shall be replayed (not cancelling any prior fault serve).

RULE 6. FAULT SERVES
The following serves are faults and any two in succession result in an out.

Rule 6. A. FOOT FAULTS
A foot fault results when:

1) The server does not begin the service motion with both feet in the service zone.

2) The server leaves the service zone before the served ball passes the short line.

3) In doubles, the server's partner is not in the service box with both feet on the floor and back to the wall from the time the server begins the service motion until the ball passes the short line.

Rule 6. B. SHORT SERVICE
A short serve is any served ball that first hits the front wall and on the rebound hits the floor on or in front of the short line (with or without touching a side wall).

Rule 6. C. THREE-WALL SERVE
Any served ball that first hits the front wall and on the rebound hits the two side walls on the fly.

Rule 6. D. CEILING SERVE
Any served ball that first hits the front wall and then touches the ceiling (with or without touching a side wall).

Rule 6. E. LONG SERVE
Any served ball that first hits the front wall and rebounds to the back wall before touching the floor (with or without touching a side wall).

Rule 6. F. OUT OF COURT SERVE
Any served ball that first hits the front wall and then goes out of the court.

RULE 7. OUT SERVES
Any of the following serves results in an out.

Rule 7. A. FAILURE OF SERVER
Failure of server to put the ball into play within ten (10) seconds of the calling of the score by the referee.

Rule 7. B. MISSED BALL
Any attempt to strike the ball that results in a total miss or in touching any part of the server's body other than the racquet.

Rule 7. C. NON-FRONT SERVE
Any served ball that does not strike the front wall first.

Rule 7. D. TOUCHED SERVE
Any served ball that on the rebound from the front wall touches the server (or server's

racquet) on a fly, or any ball intentionally stopped or caught by the server or server's partner.

Rule 7. E. CROTCH SERVE
If the served ball hits the crotch of the front wall and floor, front wall and side wall, or front wall and ceiling; it is considered "no good" and is an out serve. A serve into the crotch of the back wall and the floor is good and in play. A served ball hitting the crotch of the side wall and floor (as in a "Z" serve) beyond the short line is "good" and in play.

Rule 7. F. ILLEGAL HIT
Any illegal hit (contacting the ball twice, carries, or hitting the ball with the handle of the racquet or part of the body or uniform) results in an out serve.

Rule 7. G. FAKE OR BALK SERVE
Such a serve is defined as a non-continuous movement of the racquet towards the ball as the server drops the ball for the purpose of serving and results in an out serve.

Rule 7. H. OUT-OF-ORDER SERVE
In doubles, when either partner serves out of order, any points which may have been scored during an out of order serve will be automatically void with the score reverting to the score prior to the out of order serve. The "out serve" shall be applied to the first server and the second server shall then be allowed to serve.

RULE 8. RETURN OF SERVE
Rule 8. A. RECEIVING POSITION
The receiver(s) must stand at least five (5) feet back of the short line as indicated by the vertical line on each sidewall, and cannot enter into this safety zone until the ball has been served and passes the short line. At that point the receiver(s) may enter the safety zone to return serve, however, neither the racquet nor body may infringe on the imaginary plane marked by the short line. A violation of the receiving zone or the short line by the receiver(s) results in a point for the server.

Rule 8. B. DEFECTIVE SERVE
The receiving side shall not catch or touch a defectively served ball until a call by the referee has been made or it has touched the floor for the second time.

Rule 8. C. LEGAL RETURN
After the ball is legally served one of the players on the receiving side must strike the ball with the racquet either on the fly or after the first bounce and before the ball touches the floor the second time to return the ball to the front wall, either directly or after touching one or both sidewalls, the back wall or the ceiling, or any combination of those surfaces. A returned ball may not touch the floor before touching the front wall.

Rule 8. D. FAILURE TO RETURN
The failure to return a serve results in a point for the server.

RULE 9. CHANGES OF SERVE
Rule 9. A. OUTS
A server is entitled to continue serving until:
1) **Out serve.** The player commits an out serve as per Rule 7.
2) Player commits two fault serves in succession as per Rule 6.
3) **Hits Partner.** Player hits their partner with an attempted return.
4) **Return Failure.** Player or partner fails to hit the ball on one bounce or fails to return the ball to the front wall on a fly (with or without hitting any combination of walls and ceiling).
5) **Avoidable Hinder.** Player or partner commits an avoidable hinder as per rule 12.

Rule 9. B. SIDE OUT
In singles, a single hand-out or out, equals a side-out and retires the server. In doubles a single hand-out equals a side-out on the first service of each game; thereafter, two hand-outs equal a side-out and thereby retires the serving team.

Rule 9. C. EFFECT
When the server, or the serving team receives a side out, the server(s) become the receiver(s) and the receiver(s) become the server(s).

RULE 10. RALLIES
Each legal return after the serve is called a rally. Play during rallies shall be according to the following rules:

Rule 10. A. LEGAL HITS
Only the head of the racquet may be used at any time to return the ball. The racquet may be held in one or both hands. Switching hands to hit a ball, touching the ball with any part of the body or uniform, or removing the wrist thong result in loss of the rally.

Rule 10. B. ONE TOUCH
In attempting returns, the ball may be touched or struck only once by a player or team or the result is a loss of rally. The ball may not be "carried." (A carried ball is one which rests on the racquet in such a way that the effect is more of a "sling" or "throw" than a hit.)

Rule 10. C. FAILURE TO RETURN
Any of the following constitutes a failure to make a legal return during a rally.
1) the ball bounces on the floor more than once before being hit;
2) the ball does not reach the front wall on the fly;
3) the ball caroms off a player's racquet into a gallery or wall opening without first hitting the front wall;

4) a ball which obviously did not have the velocity or direction to hit the front wall strikes another player on the court;
5) a ball struck by one player on a team hits that player's partner, or a player is struck by a ball which was previously hit by that player, or partner.;
6) an avoidable hinder as per rule 12 is committed.

Rule 10. D.   EFFECT

Violations of Rule 10 A, B, and C result in a loss of rally. If the serving player or team loses the rally it is an "out" (handout or sideout). If the receiver(s) loses the rally, it results in a point for the server(s).

Rule 10. E.   RETURN ATTEMPTS

1) In singles, if a player swings at, but misses the ball, the player may continue to attempt to return the ball until it touches the floor for the second time.
2) In doubles, if one player swings at, but misses the ball, both partners may make further attempts to return the ball until it touches the floor the second time. Both partners on a side are entitled to return the ball.

Rule 10. F.   OUT OF COURT BALL

1) **After Return.** Any ball returned to the front wall which on the rebound or on the first bounce goes into the gallery or through any opening in a sidewall shall be declared dead and the server shall receive two serves.
2) **No Return.** Any ball not returned to the front wall, but which caroms off a player's racquet into the gallery or into any opening in a sidewall either with or without touching the ceiling, side or back wall, shall be an out or point against the player(s) failing to make the return.

Rule 10. H.   BROKEN BALL

If there is any suspicion that a ball has broken on the serve, or during a rally, play shall continue until the end of the rally. The referee or any player may request the ball be examined. If the referee decides the ball is broken, a new ball shall be put into play and the server given two serves. The only proper way to check for a broken ball is to squeeze it by hand. (Checking the ball by striking it with a racquet will not be considered a valid check and shall work to the disadvantage of the player or team which struck the ball after the rally).

Rule 10. I.   PLAY STOPPAGE

If a player loses a shoe or other equipment, or foreign objects enter the court, or any other outside interference occurs, the referee shall stop the play, if such occurrences interfere with ensuing play or player's safety.

Rule 10. J.   REPLAYS

Any rallies which are replayed for any reason without the awarding of a point or sideout shall result in any previous faults being cancelled and the server awarded two serves.

RULE 11.   DEAD BALL HINDERS

Dead ball hinders result in the rally being replayed without penalty and the server receiving two serves.

Rule 11. A.   SITUATIONS

1) **Court hinders.** A ball that hits any part of the court which has been designated as a court hinder, or any ball that takes an irregular bounce off a rough or irregular surface in such a manner as the referee determines that said irregular bounce affected the rally.
2) **Hitting Opponent.** Any returned ball that touches an opponent on the fly before it returns to the front wall. The player that has been hit or "nicked" by the ball may make this call, but it must be made immediately and acknowledged by the referee. Any ball which hits an opponent that obviously did not have the velocity or direction to reach the front wall shall not result in a hinder (and shall cause the player or team that hit the ball to lose the rally).
3) **Body Contact.** If body contact occurs which the referee believes was sufficient to stop the rally, either for the purpose of preventing injury by further contact or because the contact prevented a player from being able to make a reasonable return, the referee shall award a hinder. Body contact, particularly on the follow-through, is not necessarily a hinder.
4) **Screen ball.** Any ball rebounding from the front wall close to the body of a player on the side which just returned the ball which interferes with or prevents the returning player or side from seeing the ball.
5) **Back Swing Hinder.** Any body contact either on the back swing or en route to or just prior to returning the ball which impairs the hitter's ability to take a reasonable swing. This call may be made by the player attempting to return if it is made immediately and it is subject to acceptance and approval of the referee.
6) **Safety Holdup.** Any player about to execute a return who believes they are likely to strike their opponent with the ball or racquet may immediately stop play and request a dead ball hinder. This call must be made immediately and is subject to acceptance and approval of the referee. (The referee will grant a

dead ball hinder if he believes the holdup was reasonable and the player would have been able to return the shot, and the referee may also determine to call an avoidable hinder if warranted.)

7) **Other Interference.** Any other unintentional interference which prevents an opponent from having a fair chance to see or return the ball.

Rule 11. B. EFFECT

A call by the referee of a "hinder" stops the play and voids any situation following (such as the ball hitting a player). The only hinders a player may call are specified in Rules 11 A. 2), 11 A. 5), and 11 A. 6) and are subject to the acceptance of the referee. The effect of a dead ball hinder is that the player who served shall serve again, and shall be awarded two serves.

Rule 11. C. AVOIDANCE

While making an attempt to return the ball, a player is entitled to a fair chance to see and return the ball. It is the responsibility of the side that has just served or returned the ball to move so the receiving side may go straight to the ball and have an unobstructed view of the ball after it leaves the front wall. In the judgment of the referee however, the receiver must make a reasonable effort to move towards the ball and have a reasonable chance to return the ball in order for a hinder to be called.

RULE 12. AVOIDABLE HINDERS

An avoidable hinder results in the loss of a rally. An avoidable hinder does not necessarily have to be an "intentional" act and is a result of any of the following:

Rule 12. A. FAILURE TO MOVE

Does not move sufficiently to allow an opponent a shot.

Rule 12. B. BLOCKING

Moves into a position effecting a block on the opponent about to return the ball, or in doubles, one partner moves in front of an opponent as the partner of that opponent is returning the ball.

Rule 12. C. MOVING INTO THE BALL

Moves in the way and is struck by the ball just played by the opponent.

Rule 12. D. PUSHING

Deliberately pushes or shoves opponent during a rally.

Rule 12. E.

Moves so as to restrict opponent's swing so that the player returning the ball does not have a free unimpeded swing.

Rule 12. F. INTENTIONAL DISTRACTIONS

Deliberate shouting, stamping of feet, waving of racquet, or any manner of disrupting the player who is hitting the ball.

Rule 12. G. WETTING THE BALL

The players, particularly the server, have the responsibility to see that the ball is kept dry at all times. Any wetting of the ball either deliberate or by accident, that is not corrected prior to the beginning of the rally shall result in an avoidable hinder.

RULE 13. TIME OUTS

Rule 13. A. REST PERIODS

During games to 21, each player or team is allowed up to three (3) thirty-second time-outs (2 per side in games to 11). Time outs may not be called by either party after the server begins the service motion.

Rule 13. B. INJURY

If a player is injured during the course of a match as a result of contact with the ball, racquet, opponent, wall or floor they shall be granted an injury time-out. An injured player shall not be allowed more than a total of 15 minutes of rest during the match. If the injured player is not able to resume play after total rest of 15 minutes, the match shall be awarded to the opponent(s). Muscle cramps and pulls, fatigue, and other ailments that are not caused by direct contact on the court will not be considered an "injury".

Rule 13. C. EQUIPMENT TIME-OUTS

Players are expected to keep all clothing and equipment in good, playable condition and are expected to use regular time outs and time between games for adjustment and replacement of equipment. If a player or team is out of time outs and the referee determines that an equipment change or adjustment is necessary for fair and safe continuation of the match, the referee may award an equipment time-out not to exceed two minutes.

Rule 13. D. BETWEEN GAMES

A five minute rest period is allowed between all games of a match.

Rule 13. E. POSTPONED GAMES

Any games postponed by referees shall be resumed with the same score as when postponed.

RULE 14. TECHNICALS

Rule 14. A. TECHNICAL FOULS

The referee is empowered to deduct one point from a player's or team's score when in the referee's sole judgment, the player is being overtly and deliberately abusive. The actual invoking of this penalty is called a "Referee's Technical". If after the technical is called against the abusing player, and the

play is not immediately continued, the referee is empowered to forfeit the match in favor of the abusing player's opponent(s). Some examples of actions which may result in technicals are:
1) Profanity. Profanity is an automatic technical and should be invoked by the referee whenever it occurs.
2) Excessive Arguing.
3) Threat of any nature to opponent(s) or referee.
4) Excessive or hard striking of the ball between rallies.
5) Slamming of the racquet against walls or floor; slamming the door, or any action which might result in injury to the court or other player(s).
6) Delay of game, either in the form of taking too much time during time-outs and between games, in drying the court, in excessive questioning of the referee on the rules, or in excessive or unnecessary appeals.
7) Anything considered to be unsportsmanlike behavior.

Rule 14. B. TECHNICAL WARNING

If a player's behavior is not so severe as to warrant a "referee's technical", a technical warning may be issued without point deduction.

Rule 14. C. EFFECT

If a referee issues a Technical Warning, it shall not result in a loss of rally or point and shall be accompanied by a brief explanation of the reason for the warning. If a referee issues a Referee's Technical, one point shall be removed from the offender's score. The awarding of the technical shall have no effect on service changes or side-outs. If the technical occurs either between games or when the offender has no points, the result will be that the offender's score will revert to a minus one (-1).

RULE 15. PROFESSIONAL

A professional shall be defined as any player (male, female or junior) who has accepted prize money regardless of the amount in any PRO SANCTIONED tournament. (WPRA, CATALINA) or any other association so deemed by the AARA Board of Directors.
1) A player may **participate** in a PRO SANCTIONED tournament which awards cash prizes, but will not be considered a professional if NO prize money is accepted.
2) The acceptance by a player of merchandise or travel expenses shall not be considered as prize money, and thus does not jeopardize a player's amateur status.

RULE 16. RETURN TO AMATEUR STATUS

Any player who has been classified as a professional (see Rule 15) can recover amateur status by requesting, in writing, this desire to be reclassified as an amateur. This application shall be tendered to the Executive Director of the American Amateur Racquetball Association and shall become effective immediately as long as the player making application for reinstatement of amateur status has received NO money for the course of that year.

RULE 17. AGE GROUP DIVISIONS

Age is determined as of the first day of the tournament.

MEN'S AGE DIVISIONS:

Open — All players other than Pro
Junior Veterans Open — Amateurs 25+
Veterans Open — Amateurs 30+
Seniors — Amateurs 35+
Veteran Seniors — Amateurs 40+
Masters — Amateurs 45+
Veteran Masters — Amateurs 50+
Golden Masters — Amateurs 55 +
Senior Golden Masters — Amateurs 60+
Veteran Golden Masters — Amateurs 65+

WOMEN'S AGE DIVISIONS:

Open — All players other than Pro
Junior Veterans Open — Amateurs 25+
Veterans Open — Amateurs 30+
Seniors — Amateurs 35+
Veteran Seniors — Amateurs 40+
Masters — Amateurs 45+
Veteran Masters — Amateurs 50+
Golden Masters — Amateurs 55 +
Senior Golden Masters — Amateurs 60+
Veteran Golden Masters — Amateurs 65+

OTHER DIVISIONS

Mixed Doubles
Disabled

JUNIOR DIVISIONS

Age determined as of January 1st of each calendar year.

JUNIOR BOYS

18 years + under
16 years + under
14 years + under
12 years + under
10 years + under
 8 years + under (no bounce)
Double Team — ages apply as above.

JUNIOR GIRLS

18 years + under
16 years + under
14 years + under
12 years + under
10 years + under
 8 years + under (no bounce)

SCORING — All matches in Junior divisions will be the best of two games to 15 points, win by 1 point. If a tie breaker 3rd game is necessary the game is played to 15 points win by 2 points up to 21 points win by 1 point.

Junior Players should abide by all AARA rules with the following exceptions:

Rule 17. A. EYEGUARDS
Eyeguards *must* be worn in all AARA sanctioned events.

Rule 17. B. TIMEOUTS
Three in each game.

4 — TOURNAMENTS

RULE 18. DRAWS
a) If possible, all draws shall be made at least two (2) days before the tournament commences. The seeding method of drawing shall be approved by the American Amateur Racquetball Association.
b) The draw and seeding committee shall be chaired by the AARA's Executive Director, National Commissioner, and the host Tournament Director. No other persons shall participate in the draw or seeding unless at the invitation of the draw and seeding committee.
c) In local, state and regional tournaments the draw shall be the responsibility of the tournament chairperson. In regional play the tournament chairperson should work in coordination with the AARA Regional Commissioner at the tournament.

Rule 19. SCHEDULING
a) Preliminary Matches. If one or more contestants are entered in both singles and doubles, they may be required to play both singles and doubles on the same day or night with little rest between matches. This is a risk assumed on entering both singles and doubles events. If possible the schedule should provide at least one hour rest period between matches.
b) Final Matches. Where one or more players has reached the finals in both singles and doubles, it is recommended that the doubles match be played on the day preceding the singles. This would assure more rest between the final matches. If both final matches must be played on the same day or night, the following procedure is recommended:
  1) The singles match be played first.
  2) A rest period of not less than one (1) hour be allowed between the finals in singles and doubles.

Rule 20. NOTICE OF MATCHES
After the first round of matches, it is the responsibility of each player to check the posted schedules to determine the time and place of each subsequent match. If any change is made in the schedule after posting, it shall be the duty of the committee or chairperson to notify the players of the change.

Rule 21. THIRD PLACE
Players are not required to play off for 3rd place or 4th place. However, for point standings, if one semifinalist wants to play off for third and the other semifinalist does not, the one willing to play shall be awarded third place. If both semifinalists do not wish to play off for 3rd and 4th positions, then the points shall be awarded evenly.

Rule 22. AARA REGIONAL TOURNAMENTS
AARA Regional Tournaments — The United States and Europe are divided into a combined total of sixteen (16) regions.
a) A player may compete in only one regional tournament per year.
b) The defined area of eligibility for a person's region is that of their permanent residence. The only exception is when the locale of the adjoining regional tournament is closer to a player's residence than the site of their own home regional. In such a case the player is afforded the option of playing in either, but not both tournaments.
c) A player can participate in only two events in a regional tournament.
d) Awards and remuneration to the AARA National Championships will be posted on the entry blank.

Rule 23. TOURNAMENT MANAGEMENT
In all AARA sanctioned tournaments the tournament director and/or the National AARA official in attendance may decide on a change of courts after the completion of any tournament game if such a change will accommodate better spectator conditions.

Rule 24. TOURNAMENT CONDUCT
In all AARA sanctioned tournaments the referee is empowered to default a match if an individual player (or team) conducts themself (itself) to the detriment of the tournament and the game.

Rule 25. AARA ELIGIBILITY
Any paid-up AARA member in good standing, who has not been classified as a professional (see Rule 4.14) may compete in any AARA sanctioned tournament.

Rule 26. AARA NATIONAL CHAMPIONSHIPS

The National Singles and National Doubles were separated and will be played on different weekends. There will be a consolation round in all divisions.

a) Qualifying Singles. A player may have to qualify at one of the sixteen (16) regional tournaments.

A.A.R.A. REGIONS

Region 1 — Maine, New Hampshire, Vermont, Massachusetts, Rhode Island, Connecticut
Region 2 — New York, New Jersey
Region 3 — Pennsylvania, Maryland, Virginia, Delaware, District of Columbia
Region 4 — Florida, Georgia, North Carolina, South Carolina
Region 5 — Alabama, Mississippi, Tennessee
Region 6 — Arkansas, Kansas, Missouri, Oklahoma
Region 7 — Texas, Louisiana
Region 8 — Wisconsin, Iowa
Region 9 — West Virginia, Ohio, Michigan
Region 10 — Illinois, Indiana, Kentucky
Region 11 — North Dakota, South Dakota, Minnesota, Nebraska
Region 12 — Arizona, New Mexico, Utah, Colorado
Region 13 — Wyoming, Montana
Region 14 — Nevada, California, Hawaii
Region 15 — Washington, Idaho, Oregon, Alaska
Region 16 — Americans in Europe

1) The National Ratings Committee may handle the rating of each region and determine how many players shall qualify from each regional tournament.

2) All National finalists in each division may be exempt from qualifying for the same division the following year.

3) There may be a tournament one day ahead of the National Tournament at the same site to qualify eight (8) players in each division who were unable to qualify or who failed to qualify in the Regionals.

Rule 27. INTERCOLLEGIATE TOURNAMENT

It will be conducted at a separate date and location.

5 — ONE WALL AND THREE WALL RULES

Rule 28. ONE WALL AND THREE WALL RULES

Basically racquetball rules for one-wall, three-wall and four-wall are the same with the following exception:

One Wall: Court Size — Wall shall be 20 ft. in width and 16 ft. high, floor 20 ft. in width and 34 ft. from the wall to the back edge of the long line. There should be a minimum of three (3) feet beyond the long line and six (6) feet outside each side line and behind the long line to permit movement area for the players.

Short Line — Back edge sixteen (16) feet from the wall.

Service Markers — Lines at least six (6) inches long parallel to and midway between the long and short lines, extending in from the side lines. The imaginary extension and joining of these lines indicates the service line. Lines are 1½ inches in width.

Service Zone — Floor area inside and including the short, side and service lines.

Receiving Zone — Floor area in back of short line bounded by and including the long and side lines.

Three Wall Serve — A serve that goes beyond the side walls on the fly, is considered "long." A serve that goes beyond the long line on a fly, but within the sidewalls is the same as "short."

Court Size — short sidewall — 20' in width and 20' in height and 20' in length. Sidewall shall extend back on either side from the front wall parallel 20' along the sidewall markers. Sidewall may extend from 20' at the front wall and taper down to 12' at the end of the sidewall. All other markings are the same as 4-wall.

Court Size — long sidewall — 20' in width and 20' in height and 40' in length. Sidewall shall extend back on either side 40'. The sidewall may, but is not restricted to tapering from 20' of height at the front wall down to 12'-15' at the 40' marker. All lines are the same as in 4-wall racquetball.

RULES FOR 8 & UNDER NO-BOUNCE

Use AARA Racquetball rules with these modifications:

After a legal serve, the ball may bounce as many times as the receiver wants until he (or she) swings once to return the ball to the front wall. (In other words, they get one swing at the ball to get it back!)

The ball may be hit after the serve or during a rally at any time, but *must* be hit *before* it crosses the *short line* on its way *back* to the front wall.

The receiver can hit the ball before it hits the back wall or may play it off the back wall but cannot cross the short line *after* the ball contacts the back wall.

HOW TO REF WHEN THERE IS NO REF

Rule 1 — SAFETY

SAFETY IS THE PRIMARY AND OVERRIDING RESPONSIBILITY OF EVERY PLAYER WHO ENTERS THE COURT. At *no time* should the physical safety of the participants be compromised. Players are entitled, AND EXPECTED to hold up their swing, WITHOUT PENALTY, any time they believe there might be a risk of physical contact. Any time a player says he held up to avoid contact, even if he was over cautious, he is entitled to a hinder (rally replayed without penalty).

Rule 2 — SCORE

Since there is no ref, or scorekeeper, it is important to see that there is no misunderstanding in this area, so THE SERVER IS REQUIRED to announce both the server's and receiver's score before EVERY first serve.

Rule 3 — DURING RALLIES

During rallies, it is generally the *hitter's* responsibility to make the call — if there is a possibility of a skip ball, double-bounce, or illegal hit, play should continue until the *hitter* makes the call against himself. If the hitter does not make the call against himself and goes on to win the rally, and the player thought that one of the *hitter's* shots was not good, he may "appeal" to the hitter by pointing out which shot he thought was bad and request the hitter to reconsider. If the hitter is sure of his call, AND the opponent is still sure the hitter is wrong, the rally is replayed. As a matter of etiquette, players are *expected* to make calls against themselves any time they are not sure. In other words, if a shot is very close as to whether or not it was a good kill or a skip ball, unless the hitter is *sure* the shot was good, he should call it a skip.

The only exception to crossing the short line is if the ball is returned to the back wall from the front wall on the fly (without touching the floor) then the receiver may cross the short line and play the ball on the first bounce.

New additions are lines on the front wall (use tape) at 3 ft. and 1 ft. high. If the ball is hit below the 3 ft. and above the 1 ft. lines during a rally, it has to be returned *before* it bounces the third time. If the ball hits below the 1 ft. line during a rally, it must be played or returned to the front wall before it bounces twice or

regulation racquetball. This gives incentive to keeping the ball low.

Games are played best 2 out of three games to 11 points.

Rule 4 — SERVICE

A) Fault Serves (Long, Short, Ceiling & 3-wall): The *RECEIVER* has the primary responsibility to make these calls, and again, he should give the benefit of the doubt to his opponent whenever it is close. The receiver must make his call immediately, and not wait until he hits the ball and has the benefit of seeing how good a shot he can hit. IT IS NOT AN OPTION PLAY . . . the receiver does not have the right to play a short serve just because he thinks it's a setup.

B) Screen Serves: When there is no referee, a screen serve DOES NOT BECOME AN OPTION PLAY. When the receiver believes his vision of the ball was sufficiently impaired as to give the server too great an advantage on the serve, the receiver may hold up his swing and call a screen serve, or, if he still feels he can make a good shot at the ball, he can say nothing and continue playing. HE MAY NOT CALL A SCREEN AFTER HE ATTEMPTS TO HIT THE BALL. Further, the server may not call a screen under any circumstances . . . he must simply expect to have to play the rally until he hears a call from the receiver. (In doubles, unless the ball goes behind the back of the server's partner, no screens should be called.)

C) Footfaults, 10 second violations, receiving-line violations, service-zone infringement and other "technical" calls really require a referee. HOWEVER, if either player believes his opponent is abusing any of these rules, between rallies he should discuss it with his opponent to be sure there is agreement on what the rule is, and to put each other on notice that the rules should be followed.

Rule 5 — HINDERS

Generally, the hinder should work like the screen serve — as an option play for the hindered party. *ONLY* the person going for the shot can stop play by calling a hinder, and he must do so immediately — not wait until he has the benefit of seeing how good a shot he can hit. If the hindered party believes he can make an effective return in spite of some physical contact or screen that has occurred, he may continue to play. HOWEVER, as safety is the overriding factor, EITHER PARTY may call a hinder if it is to prevent contact.

Rule 6 — AVOIDABLE HINDERS

Since avoidable hinders are usually not intentional, they do occur even in the friendliest matches. When a player turns the wrong way and gets in the way of his opponent's setup, there should be a better way than saying, "I'm sorry" to make up for the mistake. Instead of saying "I'm sorry," the player who realizes he made such an error should simply award the rally to his opponent. If a player feels his opponent was guilty of an avoidable, and the player did not call it on himself, the "offended" player should appeal to his opponent by pointing out that he thought it was an avoidable. The player may then call it on himself, or disagree, but the call can only be made on yourself. Often, just pointing out what you think is an avoidable will put the player on notice for future rallies and prevent recurrence.

Rule 7 — DISPUTES

If either player, for any reason desires to have a referee, it is considered common courtesy for the other player to go along with the request, and a referee suitable to both sides should be found. If there is not a referee, and a question about a rule or rule interpretation comes up, seek out the club pro or a more experienced player, then, after the match, contact your local state racquetball association for the answer.

Some editorial changes have been made in the body of the official rules to insure a more complete understanding of the rules.

(Reprinted with permission from the American Amateur Racquetball Association)

Index

A

American Amateur Racquetball Association, 181
aerobic conditioning, 140
    exercise heart rate, 142
    heart rate, 141
    maximum heart rate, 141
anxiety, 123
around-the-wall ball, 59
attentional focus
    broad-external, 130
    broad-internal, 130
    narrow-external, 130
    narrow-internal, 130

B

back wall, 79, 85
battleball, 79
blocking, 172

C

carbohydrates, 151
ceiling shot,
    front wall ceiling, 49
    ceiling front wall, 53
cool-down, 148
common injuries,
    care of, 149
    dehydration, 149
    electrolyte replacement solution, 150
    heat and dehydration, 149
    injuries, 148
    overheating, 149
    overuse of muscles, tendons, and ligaments, 149
    pain, 149
    swelling around joints, 149
competition, 121
competitive versus recreational tournaments, 184
concentration, 93, 131
continental grip, 21
coping skills, 124
corner shots, 87
court etiquette, 165
    application of warm-up, 165
    common faults, 166
    hinders, 167
    sportsmanship, 169
crotch shots, 176
cut-throat, 2, 177

D

defensive game, 102
defensive shots,
    around-the-wall, 59
    ceiling shot, 49, 53
    ceiling to front wall, 53
    front wall to ceiling, 49
    high Z, 57
    lob, 54
developing strength and endurance,
    calisthenics, 144
    endurance, 143
    muscle strength, 143
    weight training, 144
doubles, 2, 177
drills, 153
drop shot, 89

E

eastern,
    backhand, 17
    forehand, 15
etiquette, 165

F

fear of failure, 122
flexibility, 134, 147
flow, 122
foot movement,
    cross stepping, 22
    pivot, 21

G

grips,
    continental, 18
    eastern backhand, 17
    eastern forehand, 15
    trigger pistol, 15
    western, 19

H

high Z, 57
hinders, 167
    avoidable, 172
    court, 174
    unavoidable, 172, 174
human resources, 183

I

International Amateur Racquetball Association, 182
interpreting the rules,
    ball in play, 171
    fault, 171
    keeping score, 170
    long, 171
    service, 170
    short, 171
    side out, 171
    two walls, 171
In Review, 182

K

kill shot,
    corner kill, 37
    overhead kill, 40
    pinch kill, 38
    straight-in kill, 36

L

legal serve, 64
lob shot, 54

M

mental rehearsal, 126
moving to the ball, 100

N

National Racquetball, 182
negative attitudes, 129
non-thinking strategy,
    center court, 97
    concentration, 93
    keeping the ball in play, 102
    leaving the center court to play the ball, 100
    moving to a court position, 99
    moving to the ball, 100
    opponent's errors, 93
    patience, 103
    playing a defensive game, 102
    serve, 95

O

offensive shot, 33
officiating, 169
outfitting for play, 3
    balls, 5
    gloves, 4
    goggles, 4
    grip size, 6
    racquets, 6
    shoes, 4
    strings and tension of strings, 8

P

passing shots,
    cross-court, 45
    down-the-line, 44
    pass, 42
patience, 103
pendulum swing, 50
physical conditioning, 133
pivot, 21
progressive relaxation, 127, 168

R

racquet,
    care, 7
    grip size, 6
    tension, 7
    types, 6

Index

reaction, 146
receiving line, 1
relaxation, 13, 124, 147

S

safety,
    collision, 10
    diving, 10
    goggles, 12
    hinder, 8
    hitting ball into the back wall, 12
    thong, 7, 9
service zone, 1
serving,
    drive, 68
    garbage, 75
    half lob, 68
    high Z, 70
    legal serve, 2, 64
    lob, 66
    overhead, 73
    Z, 70
set position, 20
sportsmanship, 169
stretching, 15
    hold the stretch position, 155
strokes,
    backhand, 27
    forehand, 22

T

tension, 124
thinking strategy,
    anticipation, 109
    best offense against a power
        player, 118
    blocking, 114
    choosing the right serve, 105
    concentration, 93
thinking strategy,
    controlling the tempo, 109
    hitting a winning shot, 115
    hit to the farthest corner, 116
    hit your hardest serve, 107
    hustle, 119
    keeping the opponent moving, 113
    moving the opponent out of
        the center court, 114
    moving to cut off the opponent's
        return, 119
    opponent's backhand, 105
    returning to the offense, 113
    shot returns, 110
    take away opponent's
        best shot, 112
    using the court wisely, 112
    variety in your shot, 105
trigger grip, 15
tournaments,
    college, 184
    competitive versus recreational
        tournament play, 184

U

use of the back wall, 79, 85

V

volley shots, 90

W

warm-up, 13, 146
    cool-down, 148
    etiquette, 165
    increase heart rate, 16, 148
western grip, 19
wrist,
    cock, 23, 28
    snap, 25, 29, 91